Ronald Reagan's
AMERICA

⋆ His Voice, His Dreams, *and* His Vision *of* Tomorrow ⋆

TERRY GOLWAY

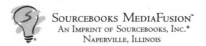
SOURCEBOOKS MEDIAFUSION™
AN IMPRINT OF SOURCEBOOKS, INC.®
NAPERVILLE, ILLINOIS

Published by Sourcebooks MediaFusion, an imprint of Sourcebooks, Inc.

P.O. Box 4410, Naperville, Illinois 60567-4410

(630) 961–3900

Fax: (630) 961–2168

www.sourcebooks.com

Library of Congress Cataloging-in-Publication Data

Golway, Terry

Ronald Reagan's America : his voice, his dreams, and his vision of tomorrow / Terry Golway.

p. cm.

Accompanying audio CD contains numerous speeches and addresses given by Ronald Reagan between 1964 and 1989.

Includes bibliographical references and index.

1. Reagan, Ronald--Political and social views. 2. Presidents--United States--Biography. 3. United States--Politics and government--1981-1989. 4. United States--Politics and government--1981-1989--Sources. I. Title.

E877.G65 2008

973.927092--dc22

[B]

2008016118

Printed and bound in the United States of America.

BG 10 9 8 7 6 5 4 3 2 1

Contents

On the CD

The audio on the accompanying compact disc has been selected by the author to enrich the your enjoyment of this book, to allow you to experience the words of Ronald Reagan in his own voice. These selections represent some of the most remarkable moments of his presidency and offer a window to the mind of the man. At the start of each chapter in the book, you will find an icon and track number denoting the corresponding speech on the CD. We encourage you to use and we hope you enjoy this mixed-media presentation of the life of Ronald Reagan.

1: National Television Address on Behalf of Barry Goldwater • *October 27, 1964*

2: Speech at the University of Southern California • *April 19, 1966*

3: Speech to the 1976 Republican National Convention • *August 19, 1976*

4: Acceptance Speech at the Republican National Convention • *July 17, 1980*

5: Debate with President Jimmy Carter • *October 28, 1980*

6: Ronald Reagan's First Inaugural Address • *January 20, 1981*

7: The First Speech after the Assassination Attempt • *April 28, 1981*

8: Press Conference on the Air Controllers' Strike • *August 3, 1981*

9: Remarks to the National Press Club on Arms Reduction • *November 18, 1981*

10: Address to the British Parliament • *June 8, 1982*

11: Address to the Nation on the Economy • *October 13, 1982*

12: Speech to the National Association of Evangelicals • *March 8, 1983*

13: Address to the Nation on Defense and National Security • *March 23, 1983*

President Reagan celebrates with his staff in the Oval Office early in his first term as president. From left to right: Richard Williamson, Elizabeth Dole, Dennis Thomas, Don Regan, Ann McLaughlin, Ed Meese, George Bush, Karna Small, David Gergen, and Ronald Reagan.

Ronald Reagan in Dixon, Illinois, during the 1920s

Ronald W. Reagan
An American Life

RONALD WILSON REAGAN WAS BORN ON FEBRUARY 6, 1911, IN THE SMALL town of Tampico, Illinois, the fourth child of John ("Jack") Reagan and Nelle Wilson Reagan. The future president's father was a salesman and a storyteller, the descendant of Irish Catholic immigrants from County Tipperary. Nelle Wilson's roots were in Scotland and England, and she worshipped at the local Disciples of Christ church. They married in 1904, at a time when matches between Catholics and Protestants were unusual and discouraged. Ronald was baptized into his mother's faith at the age of twelve, but his older brother, Neil, was raised a Catholic.

The Reagans bounced around a great deal as Jack moved from job to job. They settled in Dixon, Illinois, in 1920 when Jack and a business partner opened a shoe store in the thriving town of ten thousand people. Reagan's years in Dixon were formative: it was there, he later wrote, that he learned the values of family and hard work. Dixon, in Reagan's memory, was an idyllic place for a young boy. Outdoor life centered on the Rock River, which flowed through the center of town. It was his swimming pool in summer and his skating rink in winter.

He was an introverted child, as might be expected of one who moved often. In recalling his youth in his autobiography, Reagan mentions the names of very few of his childhood companions. In later years, biographers and observers would note that while Reagan was an amiable, charming man, he did not have many close friends. Reagan admitted as much himself, saying that he never really lost his childhood reluctance to let friends get too close to him. He never knew when it would be time to pick up and leave again.

His father was an alcoholic who disappeared for stretches at a time, almost always when times were good. Nelle explained to her children that their father had an illness, and there was nothing he could do about it. Not long afterward, when he was eleven years old, Ronald came home to find his father passed out in the snow near the front door of their home. He dragged Jack, reeking of whiskey, into the house, but never mentioned the incident to his mother.

He disliked the name Ronald—it wasn't rugged enough, he later explained. His father called him "the Dutchman" because of his Dutch-boy haircut, and so Ronald became "Dutch." The family continued to move around, even within Dixon, where they lived in five homes, owning none of them. They were a family constantly on the move.

As young Dutch entered his teenage years, he was small (about 5 feet 3 inches tall, and less than 110 pounds) and not especially gifted in sports, in part because of poor eyesight. But he loved football, and worked hard enough to earn a place on his high school team as a sophomore. He grew dramatically during his junior year, to just under 6 feet and 160 pounds By his senior year, he was a starter on the offensive line.

He also put his physique to work as a lifeguard on the shores of Lowell Park near Dixon. He became something of a legend on the lake for his dramatic rescues. The local newspaper reported in August 1928 that seventeen-year-old Dutch Reagan had saved a drowning man after another lifeguard had failed to make the rescue.

It was during these formative years that Reagan developed a taste for acting. Although he had some acting experience at a young age, when his mother persuaded him to read aloud to her church group, he developed a passion for performing in his high school English class. He relished the chance to read his own essays aloud, leading him to join the school's various stage productions.

In the fall of 1928, Reagan went off to college, a rare experience for most young men—rarer still for young women—in the 1920s. Just over 5 percent of high school seniors continued their education at the time. Reagan was admitted to Eureka College, which was run by the Disciples of Christ. It was a tiny school, with about two hundred and fifty students, and relatively close to home, just over a hundred miles from Dixon. He was given a needs-based partial scholarship due to the family's modest income.

The stock market crashed during Reagan's sophomore year, and for the rest of his college days, the Great Depression cast its terrible shadow across the nation. Reagan managed to stay in school despite the hardships. He played on the football team, swam, ran track, worked on the school year-book, served in the student senate, and did his best to maintain the C average required of student-athletes. He majored in economics, because after college he believed he'd go into business.

As the Depression worsened and Franklin Roosevelt prepared to challenge President Herbert Hoover in the 1932 presidential election, Ronald Reagan was awarded a degree in economics from Eureka College. His job prospects were minimal at best. He developed an interest in radio, the new mass medium of the age, but met with no luck when he looked for a job as an announcer in Chicago. He did, however, catch on as a college football broadcaster in the fall of 1932, earning five dollars a game at first, but doubling his pay after a few weeks. Soon he was offered a full-time job as an announcer for a radio station in Iowa with the call letters WHO.

Ronald Reagan cast his first presidential vote that year, for Franklin Roosevelt. His father voted for FDR too. When the Democrats won the White House, Jack Reagan was given a job as a relief administrator in Dixon. Ronald Reagan would cast three more votes for Franklin Roosevelt. He was a staunch New Dealer—he had seen the effects of the Depression on the Midwest, and knew what it was like to be without work. Roosevelt delivered hope and optimism, in addition to programs designed to alleviate the nation's suffering. Ronald Reagan wholeheartedly approved.

During the 1930s, Reagan's radio career took off. His became a familiar voice across the Midwest as he sat in a studio and recreated Chicago Cubs baseball games based on information sent via telegraph from the ballpark to the station. It required extraordinary imagination and an endless reserve of easy chatter. Beginning in 1935, Dutch Reagan took his act on the road, traveling to Southern California in the late winter—the timing was no coincidence—to cover the Cubs in spring training.

During his sojourn in 1937, Reagan visited the studios of Republic Pictures. It reminded him of his long-suppressed ambition to be an actor. A friend called an agent, Reagan visited the agent (after first removing his thick glasses), the agent called Warner Brothers, and Reagan was given a screen test. Duty called, however, and Reagan left Hollywood to return to his job in Iowa without waiting to hear from the studio. When he arrived in Davenport, however, a telegram from his agent awaited: Warner Brothers wanted to hire him for two hundred dollars a week for seven years. Reagan told his agent to sign the deal before the studio changed its mind. He started in June 1937.

His first starring role was as a radio announcer—he certainly was qualified for the part—in a film called *Love Is on the Air*, which was completed in three weeks. It was the beginning of a career that would span from the Depression to the Kennedy administration, one that would bring him fame and wealth that even he could not have imagined when he was looking for work in 1932.

He churned out a series of forgettable roles until his first big break, when he played the role of George Gipp, a football legend at the University of Notre Dame who died in 1920 at the age of twenty-five. The film, *Knute Rockne—All American*, told the story of Gipp's equally legendary coach, Knute Rockne, who was killed in a plane crash in 1941. Reagan's new friend, Pat O'Brien, played Rockne, and delivered the film's most memorable line: "Let's win one for the Gipper." The line became associated with Reagan, even though it was O'Brien who spoke the words. His success in the role of George Gipp helped land him a starring role in *Kings Row*, perhaps the best movie Reagan ever made.

Reagan married actress Jane Wyman in 1940 and the couple had two children, Maureen and Michael. Shortly after Reagan's success in *Knute Rockne*, his father died at the age of fifty-eight, having spent the last months of his life answering his son's fan mail. Nelle would outlive her husband by twenty-one years, but she never experienced the joy of seeing her son's continued success and fame. She died after living in the shadows for years, suffering from Alzheimer's disease.

When the United States entered World War II in 1941, Reagan already was in uniform as an officer in the Army Reserves. His poor eyesight, however, limited his duties, and when he was mobilized for active service, he was ruled ineligible for combat duty. He was assigned to the Signal Corps, where he made war movies and narrated training films for use by bomber pilots and their crews.

After the war, Reagan resumed his film career and threw himself into union politics as a member, and eventually as president, of the Screen Actors Guild. He was busy and in demand, prepared to build on the success of his prewar roles. Even so, his marriage to Wyman fell apart, and the two divorced in 1948.

As leader of the Screen Actors Guild, Reagan resisted attempts by Communists in Hollywood to win control of other film-related unions. He would later write that the experience was "eye-opening."[1] By the same token, however, some of his friends, including James Cagney and Humphrey Bogart, were falsely accused of Communist sympathies during the burgeoning Red Scare in Washington. So while Reagan was becoming an adamant anti-Communist, he also saw the effects of irrational anti-Communism on the reputations of real people. Decades later, some anti-Communists would denounce him for his historic partnership with Soviet leader Mikhail Gorbachev, making the familiar charge that he betrayed his country and his principles.

Reagan made twenty-two movies after the war, but as the 1950s progressed, roles were becoming harder to come by. In 1952, Reagan married actress Nancy Davis in front of three witnesses. They had two children, Patti and Ron Jr. To help pay the bills, Reagan took a two-week gig in Las Vegas and turned up as a frequent guest on the newest innovation in popular entertainment—television programs. Those guest spots caught the attention of executives at General Electric, who wanted to establish a GE presence on television. They approached Reagan in 1954 with an offer to host a regular weekly television show to be called the *General Electric Theater*. The show would feature well-known actors and actresses in original, one-hour dramas, with Reagan serving as the face of the series.

In addition to his television work, Reagan served as a roving ambassador for GE, touring plants around the nation and delivering a set-piece speech that began to evolve as Reagan's own politics evolved through the 1950s. After battling Communists in Hollywood's unions, Reagan's politics began to move to the right as he questioned his old loyalties to New Deal programs and big government. His standard speech, which he wrote himself, began to include critiques of government inefficiency and regulations, and praise for the spirit of unfettered private enterprise. His audience expanded beyond GE plants to include local civic and business groups.

The GE speech, with its warning that it was a slippery slope from big government to totalitarianism, became the founding document in the Reagan Revolution. He delivered it, or a version of it, hundreds of times, to audiences of blue-collar workers, small business owners, and politically connected executives. It marked the beginning of Reagan's political career, although he was years away from running for office. Still president of the Screen Actors Guild, Reagan led a strike against Hollywood's studios in 1960. That same year, he broke with the Democratic Party and endorsed Richard Nixon for president. It seemed contradictory: he was a union leader who took his members out on strike, and yet he also supported a Republican presidential candidate who was not popular with labor and who seemed, like his party, more in tune with the concerns of business than with labor. But as time would show, Ronald Reagan was more flexible and more complex than many of his critics realized.

The GE speech and his increasingly high profile as a political activist got the attention of Republicans in California. Reagan enrolled in the party in 1962, campaigned for Barry Goldwater's doomed presidential candidacy in 1964—delivering a version of the GE speech in a televised commercial pitch for Goldwater—and in 1966, he decided to run for governor of California. Few gave him a chance against the veteran incumbent, Edmund (Pat) Brown, but Reagan campaigned vigorously, promised to put an end to demonstrations on California's restive college campuses, and condemned urban disorder. It was a winning message. Reagan stunned Brown and the nation's political establishment by winning in a landslide, taking 58 percent of the vote.

He served two terms, declining to run for a third in 1974. But he was now a national political figure, the titular head of a fledgling movement that wished to move the Republican Party to the right, away from the centrist policies of Richard Nixon and other establishment figures. In 1976, Reagan decided to challenge incumbent President Gerald Ford, who took office when Nixon resigned in 1974, for that year's Republican presidential nomination. It was an audacious gamble on Reagan's part: incumbent presidents were rarely challenged from within their own party. Ford had the party's establishment and the prestige of the White House in his favor. Nevertheless, Reagan pressed on, forcing Ford on the defensive through the long primary season. When the votes were counted at the Republican convention in Kansas City, Missouri, Ford barely managed a first-ballot victory with 1,187 votes to Reagan's 1,070. The victorious president invited Reagan to the podium, a magnanimous gesture that allowed Reagan a chance to speak extemporaneously about his campaign, and his values. It was clear that at age sixty-five, Ronald Reagan still had plans for the future—his own, and the nation's.

Ford lost the general election to a Democratic newcomer named Jimmy Carter, a one-term governor of Georgia. The sense of hope that Carter brought to Washington soon faded as the nation's economy stagnated. Abroad, American prestige sunk to a post–World War II low when Iranian students seized the American embassy in Teheran and held its staff hostage. On November 13, 1979, Ronald Reagan declared that he would run for president in the 1980 primaries.

Once again, few took him very seriously. The Republican establishment's candidate was George H.W. Bush of Texas. But the Republican Party was changing at the grass-roots level, and Reagan and his supporters understood party members' yearning for a more ideological message. Reagan defeated Bush in the New Hampshire primary and never looked back. He asked Bush to serve as his vice president, and he went on to defeat Carter—after a memorable debate with the incumbent—in the general election. Reagan took slightly more than half the popular vote in a three-way race with Carter and Congressman John Anderson, an independent Republican. But in the electoral college, Reagan remade the face of American politics, taking 489 electoral votes to Carter's 44, burying for good the coalition built by the man he once idolized, Franklin Roosevelt.

Ronald Reagan took office on January 20, 1981. By the time he left, on January 20, 1989, the nation and the world had been transformed. The American economy had been revived. The nation's military was better positioned to project power overseas. Incredibly, the conflict that defined so much of his worldview, the Cold War, drew to a close during his eight years in office.

These achievements, and others, allowed Ronald Reagan to deliver a triumphant farewell address before he left office as the first two-term president since Dwight Eisenhower. Through the power of words and images, with the force of his own sunny personality, Ronald Reagan had led the nation on an unforgettable and tumultuous journey through the 1980s. He was dubbed "the great communicator" for his ability to articulate his ideas and, even more important, to persuade his fellow citizens that his way was best for the country. But he was not a natural orator like Hubert Humphrey, and his speeches, for the most part, lacked the splendid poetry of John F. Kennedy's major presidential speeches. Except when angry, as he was when he visited the Berlin wall, Reagan's tone tended to be flat and soft. His delivery was smooth, unlike the machine-gun staccato of Kennedy or Congressman Jack Kemp, but it lacked the drama of Barbara Jordan, the congresswoman from Texas, or Mario Cuomo, the governor of New York.

Unlike those more accomplished orators, however, Reagan understood that intimacy could be just as powerful as bombast, and ideas simply expressed could move a nation faster than complicated argument. Reagan's best speeches were like Franklin Roosevelt's fireside chats. They sounded like a conversation between two friends. They made expansive use of the second person—you, the listener, were part of the speech. Indeed, Reagan used moving anecdotes from the lives of ordinary Americans to illustrate his points, rather than rely on government statistic and studies. Op-Ed commentators and policy analysts disapproved of the technique, arguing that policy by anecdote was a bad idea, but for Reagan, anecdotes were a way of connecting his ideas to the lives of real people.

He understood their problems. He cast himself through his speeches as the eternal outsider who happened to be in positions of power. Red tape and bureaucratic wrangling baffled him, too. He conveyed a sense that he understood the public's frustration, as well as its greatest hopes.

Because he spoke about ideas, and because the Reagan years in Washington were more about argument than they were about great events, his speeches sometimes lack the dramatic background of Kennedy's or Roosevelt's. But what they lacked in drama, they made up for in sincerity. Even his critics conceded that Reagan believed what he said, even on those occasions when his anecdotes fell apart, or his statistics proved faulty. Ironically, again, the ideas he championed as president were not the ideas he supported as a young man. But the nation accepted his transformation, and in doing so, transformed itself.

In 1994, the former president announced that he was suffering from Alzheimer's disease, the very ailment that debilitated his mother. The nation he loved greeted the announcement with sorrow and regret. He faded away, out of public view, until June 5, 2004, when he died in his California home.

PART ONE:

Before the White House

Ronald Reagan laughs while talking to Gerald Ford at the California Republican State Convention, 1974

Introduction

IN A SENSE, RONALD REAGAN WAS HARDLY A NEWCOMER TO POLITICS WHEN HE ran for governor of California in 1966, his first bid for elective office. During his years in Hollywood, he was a frequent guest on the campaign trail, using his celebrity to hawk votes for candidates he supported. In 1948, still very much a New Deal Democrat, Reagan campaigned for Harry Truman, and two years later, he publicly supported Helen Gahagan Douglas in her epic race against Richard Nixon for a U.S. Senate seat from California. Nixon, of course, won that race.

His interest in politics grew during the 1950s, when he was president of the Screen Actors Guild. He signed a statement urging Dwight Eisenhower to run for president in 1952 as a Democrat, but when the retired general decided he was a Republican, Reagan campaigned for him anyway. It was the first sign that Reagan's political views were changing. By 1960, he was a Republican in all but name, campaigning enthusiastically for Richard Nixon while many of his show-business colleagues rallied around John Kennedy.

His career change, from actor to politician, was not particularly abrupt. His candidacy for governor in 1966 was the end product of years spent around politics and politicians. He cast himself as a citizen-politician, an average voter who rose to speak on behalf of other average voters. While he surely was not a student of state government in 1966, he also was not a rookie on the campaign trail.

He won the governor's race in 1966 in part because the two-term incumbent, Edmund (Pat) Brown, didn't take him seriously, and in part because of voter reaction to riots in Watts in 1965 and student unrest in the University of California system, particularly at Berkeley. But ideas also played a part in his victory. Reagan campaigned as an ideological candidate openly opposed to the direction of Lyndon Johnson's Great Society programs. In April 1966, Reagan told an audience at the University of Southern California of his vision for a Creative Society, in contrast to Lyndon Johnson's Great Society of social-welfare programs.

He defeated Brown with astonishing ease, winning approximately 3.4 million votes to Brown's 2.5 million. Once in office, he ordered hiring freezes and other budget reductions that did little to reduce the actual cost of government, but which symbolized his determination to change the status quo. The extent of his ambitions became clear in 1968, just two years into his tenure, when he and his supporters halfheartedly tried to wrest the Republican presidential nomination from Nixon during the party's convention in Miami.

Reagan was a national figure after his reelection in 1970. He declined to run for a third term in 1974, but he had no intention of spending the rest of his days on horseback at his ranch. Disenchanted with Gerald Ford, who became president after Richard Nixon's resignation in 1974, and worried that the United States was losing the Cold War, Reagan ran for the presidency again in 1976. He nearly succeeded in denying Ford, a sitting president, his party's nomination, but after a tumultuous primary season, Ford prevailed in one of the most contested conventions of recent times.

Reagan turned sixty-five in 1976, and many political observers believed he was finished as a player in national politics. Not for the first time, and not for the last, the political establishment underestimated Reagan's tenacity and ambition. In late 1979, Ronald Reagan announced that he would be a candidate again in 1980. A half-dozen prominent Republicans already were in the field, hoping to take advantage of a stagnant economy and incumbent President Jimmy Carter's political weaknesses. Although Reagan lost the first contest of the election season, the Iowa caucus, he won in New Hampshire and went on to capture the nomination with ease.

During the general election, Carter and his supporters portrayed Reagan as a latter-day Barry Goldwater, a potentially dangerous ideologue who could not be trusted with the nation's highest office. Some liberal and moderate Republicans were uneasy with Reagan and the new conservative voices who supported him. Some rallied to the third-party candidacy of Republican Congressman John Anderson of Illinois.

Reagan's message, however, was not nearly as harsh as his critics contended, and in any case, voters were open to an argument in favor of change. After years of frustration abroad and hard times at home, Americans proved willing to take a chance on a candidate who spoke unapologetically of the nation's exceptionalism, of its past glories, and of its bright future.

Ronald Reagan defeated Carter and Anderson in a landslide. The Reagan Revolution was underway.

Ronald Reagan on the set of General Electric Theater

CHAPTER 1

THE Speech

National Television Address on Behalf of Barry Goldwater
October 27, 1964

TRACK 1

HOW OFTEN IN AMERICAN HISTORY HAS A SINGLE SPEECH launched a memorable career in national politics? It happened in 1896, when a little-known politician from Nebraska named William Jennings Bryan electrified the Democratic National Convention with his "Cross of Gold" speech. Bryan's speech propelled him from obscurity to his party's presidential nomination in a matter of hours—those were the days when spontaneous demonstrations at political conventions really were spontaneous. In 1984, Governor Mario Cuomo delivered a stirring keynote address at the Democratic convention in San Francisco, but he would later decline the opportunity to convert his national profile into a campaign for the White House. More recently, in 2004, an unknown Senate candidate from Illinois named Barack Obama delivered a speech about the audacity of hope during the Democratic convention in Boston. That speech put Obama on a path that led to his astonishing presidential campaign in 2008.

On the evening of October 27, 1964, a single speech turned a washed-up actor into one of the most dominant political leaders of the 20th century. His name was Ronald Wilson Reagan.

In the fall of 1964, Ronald Reagan was a midlevel celebrity with a genial stage manner and a future that seemed uncertain at best. He was no longer a leading man in Hollywood. Indeed, for a generation of younger Americans, he was better known as the host of television's *General Electric Theater* than as a onetime matinee idol. Reagan's partnership with GE had ended in 1962 after an eight-year run, prompting him to return to Hollywood to make what proved to be his last movie, *The Killers*. For the first time in his acting career, Reagan played a bad guy. The movie went nowhere.

With his career on a downward spiral, he threw himself into politics in the early 1960s, not as a candidate, but as an after-dinner speaker on the fundraising circuit. It was not a huge leap, for Reagan had always had an interest in politics. "At the end of World War II, I was a New Dealer to the core," he wrote in his autobiography. He was a member of Americans for Democratic Action, a liberal, anti-Communist organization founded in the 1940s, and he was active in his union, the Screen Actors Guild, serving five terms as president in the 1950s. "I thought government could solve all our postwar problems just as it had ended the Depression and won the war," he wrote.[1]

By the late 1950s, however, his politics began to change. Some attributed his drift rightward to his father-in-law, Loyal Davis, a conservative neurosurgeon who adopted Nancy after marrying Nancy's mother, actress Edith Luckett, when Nancy was seven years old. (Nancy's biological father abandoned the family not long after she was born, in 1921.) Nancy would later downplay her stepfather's influence on her husband, insisting that Dr. Davis was not nearly as interested in politics as many people thought. Besides, Reagan already was beginning to rethink his politics even before he met Nancy. He was appalled to discover Communist influence in some of Hollywood's unions after World War II, drawing him into a fight against Soviet attempts to manipulate American labor relations. He traveled to Britain in 1949 in the midst of the Labour Party's postwar construction of a new welfare state founded on socialist principles. The transformation left him profoundly discouraged. The welfare state, he concluded, removed the incentive to work, while government red tape sapped the energy and morale of the people. He moved a step closer to break with his own past, and his own politics.

In 1956, he supported President Dwight Eisenhower's reelection campaign, his first vote for a Republican, and then campaigned for Richard Nixon in 1960 against John Kennedy. He remained a registered Democrat, but two years later, in the midst of delivering a speech on behalf of Nixon's gubernatorial campaign in California, he officially and dramatically re-registered as a Republican. A woman in the audience provided him with the registration form.

He stepped up his activism in 1964, serving as cochairman of Barry Goldwater's presidential campaign in California and delivering a speech at the Republican National Convention in San Francisco. After the convention, as the Republican Party's chances of unseating incumbent Lyndon Johnson dwindled, Reagan stood by his candidate even as other Republicans kept their distance from Goldwater's conservative message, confrontational style, and disastrous poll numbers. When some of Goldwater's supporters asked Reagan to tape a television appearance on the candidate's behalf, he readily agreed. The campaign bought thirty minutes of airtime on NBC on October 27.

Reagan's reincarnation as a political figure began that night. In the decades to come, Reagan's admirers would refer to the television address of October 27, 1964, as THE Speech, the speech that launched one of the nation's most memorable political careers, the speech that put Reagan on an improbable journey to Sacramento and then the White House. Reagan himself acknowledged that his life was transformed on that October night in 1964. The speech, he wrote in his autobiography, "was one of the most important milestones in my life."[2]

And it almost didn't happen.

A few days before the airdate, Goldwater called Reagan with some disturbing news. Some top Republicans wanted to scratch the speech because they were worried about remarks Reagan made about Social Security—he argued in favor of "voluntary features" that would keep the system on a "sound basis." Goldwater was trying to fend off Democratic assertions that if elected, his administration would abolish the popular system. Goldwater's aides didn't want him back on the defensive during the last week of his floundering campaign. So they suggested replacing the Reagan speech with an innocuous interview between the candidate and former President Dwight Eisenhower, who was basking in the glow of celebrations marking the 20th anniversary of the D-Day landings in France. Eisenhower, of course, had been the Allied Supreme Commander of the invasion.

Reagan was flabbergasted. He told Goldwater that he had been giving versions of the speech to audiences all summer and nobody had accused him of selling out the nation's elderly. Goldwater, it turned out, actually hadn't heard or seen a tape of the speech. He told Reagan he'd listen to it and then decide what to do.

In Reagan's telling, written years later, Goldwater listened to the speech, turned to his aides, and said: "What the hell's wrong with that?"[3]

The Eisenhower interview remained on the shelf. The Reagan speech went on as scheduled.

The speech was, in essence, a version of a speech Reagan had delivered many times, even before the 1964 campaign began. Reagan had long been a frequent after-dinner speaker—in Hollywood, he joked, "If you don't sing or dance, you end up an after-dinner speaker."[4] Suffice to say, unlike his friend Jimmy Cagney, Reagan had no latent song and dance skills.

By 1964, Reagan's stump speech reflected his new concerns about intrusive government, excessive regulation, the Cold War confrontation with Communism, and the importance of individual liberties. It was very much his own work, for, as biographer Lou Cannon pointed out, in the early 1960s Reagan had no speechwriters, no researchers, and no political advisors. He wrote versions of his stump speech while on long train rides—and those trips were frequent, for Reagan hated to fly.

The United States, Reagan repeatedly told his audiences, was at a crossroads: the Democratic Party had expanded government to the detriment of the very people it claimed to represent. The Republican Party was a bulwark of individual liberty and economic freedom. It was, Reagan would tell his listeners, time to choose which course the nation wished to follow. His own preference was clear.

In early fall 1964, after a handful of high-powered Republican contributors asked him to make an address supporting Goldwater, Reagan suggested a format: rather than tape a speech in a small, impersonal studio, why not deliver it in a larger venue to a preselected audience of Republican supporters?

The Goldwater supporters went along with Reagan's suggestion, so when Reagan taped the speech, he talked not only to a camera but to the kind of live audience he had been addressing for several years.

It began with the voice of an unseen announcer, who introduced Reagan as a spokesman for the Goldwater campaign. Reagan awaited his cue, looking relaxed and at ease in front of a camera, a contrast with the stiff appearances of other politicians still adjusting to a relatively new medium. The broadcast was in black and white, so the television viewers couldn't see what the live audience saw: the speaker's blue eyes and matching suit coat, the brown highlights in his slick pompadour, and his Hollywood tan. This was no ordinary political broadcast. This was a television show, hosted by a familiar face.

"I have spent most of my life as a Democrat," he said after his opening remarks. "I recently have seen fit to follow another course." Why had this onetime supporter of Franklin Roosevelt changed sides to oppose the reelection of Lyndon Johnson, a political child of the New Deal? He said he had an "uncomfortable feeling" that the nation's prosperity was little more than an illusion financed by taxes and deficit spending. Choices had to be made, and he had made his. But his argument was not just about partisan politics, about Democrat or Republican, left or right. The choice to be made was up or down, "up to a man's age-old dream, the ultimate in individual freedom consistent with law and order, or down to the ant heap of totalitarianism." The nation's current leaders, "regardless of their sincerity, their humanitarian motives" were leading the nation "on this downward course."

Reagan's message was as ideological as anything Goldwater was saying, but Reagan's delivery was smooth and unthreatening. He criticized Democrats by name—Senator William Fulbright of Arkansas, vice presidential candidate Hubert Humphrey—and portrayed them as crypto-socialists who believed in a powerful federal government, "the very thing the Founding Fathers sought to minimize." This was an extraordinary charge coming from a man who voted for Franklin Roosevelt four times, but Reagan's ideological journey was by now complete. He was convinced that the program he supported for years was leading the country to what he would later call a "silent form of socialism."[5]

Strong and expansive federal government led to high taxes, he said, and they were not just a nuisance but also a threat to the nation's existence. For there was another threat as well—Communism. In stark terms, Reagan laid out the stakes in the twilight struggle. "We are at war with the most dangerous enemy that has ever faced mankind in his long climb from the swamp to the stars," he said, "and it has been said if we lose that war, and in doing so lose this way of freedom of ours, history will record with the greatest astonishment that those who had the most to lose did the least to prevent its happening."

The implication was clear: advocates of big government, while sincere, were leading the United States on a path to Soviet-style totalitarianism. Rather than seeking victory over the Communist threat, Democrats were looking for accommodation. Americans had to choose which course they would take—the illusion of peace through appeasement, or a grim determination to resist the spread of Communism. He moved seamlessly from a critique of those who advocated accommodation to a discussion of the "martyrs of history," including Jesus Christ and the minutemen at Concord Bridge. Had a shouting, shrill Goldwater delivered those words, Democrats would have had more material to use in their effort to marginalize the Republican senator as a dangerous and perhaps unstable man. But Reagan's soft delivery and his genial charisma took the edges off talk about martyrdom and resistance. He was not so easily dismissed as a crank or a fanatic.

On issues closer to home, Reagan introduced rhetorical techniques that would become a staple in later speeches: drawing on anecdotes to illustrate the depredations of big government, he spoke of a married, pregnant mother of six who sought a divorce so she could qualify for more money on welfare, and of a farmer who "overplanted his rice allotment" and lost his farm to federal regulators who sought to make an example of him.

"Our natural, inalienable rights are now considered to be a dispensation of government, and freedom has never been so fragile, so close to slipping from our grasp as it is at this moment," he said. "Our Democratic opponents seem unwilling to debate these issues. They want to make you and I believe that this is a contest between two men ... that we are to choose just between two personalities."

But, Reagan argued, the choice was not about personality, but about ideas. He accused Democrats of seeking to destroy Goldwater, a man who, he said, "took time out [from the campaign] to sit beside an old friend who was dying of cancer" despite the wishes of his campaign aides. "This is not a man who could carelessly send other people's sons to war. And that is the issue of this campaign that makes all of the other problems I have discussed academic, unless we realize that we are in a war that must be won."

More than high taxes, more than the abuses of the welfare system, more than arguments about farm subsidies, the struggle against Communism formed the framework of the speech. Reagan returned to the theme again as he neared his conclusion. "You and I know and do not believe that life is so dear and peace so sweet as to be purchased at the price of chains and slavery," he said. "You and I have the courage to say to our enemies, 'There is a price we will not pay.'" That was Goldwater's point, he said, just as it was Winston Churchill's a quarter-century earlier.

He finished with a phrase first uttered by another World War II leader, Franklin Roosevelt. "You and I have a rendezvous with destiny," he said, echoing the words of FDR in his first inaugural. "We will preserve for our children this, the last best hope of man on Earth, or we will sentence them to take the last step into a thousand years of darkness." It was a stark choice, but it was choice that had to be made.

Ronald and Nancy Reagan watched the speech that night with friends. Reagan went to bed that night uncertain whether his performance helped or hurt Barry Goldwater. He received his answer at around midnight, California time. An aide to the Goldwater campaign called to say that calls were pouring into the candidate's headquarters. The speech was an instant hit; it was replayed throughout the country and helped raise eight million dollars for Goldwater's doomed campaign. Ronald Reagan's political career had begun.

Ronald and Nancy Reagan in Los Angeles at the celebration of Reagan's victory in the California gubernatorial race

CHAPTER 2

The Creative Society

*Speech at the University
of Southern California*
April 19, 1966

TRACK 2

RONALD REAGAN SPENT MANY DAYS IN THE SUMMER AND FALL OF 1965 driving from speech to speech up and down the California coast, testing the waters for a gubernatorial campaign in 1966. Barry Goldwater's disastrous defeat in 1964 might have been a blow for the Republican Party's fledgling conservative movement, but Reagan emerged from the wreckage as a political star in the making. Everyone—including his daughter Maureen—wanted him to run for governor against incumbent Edmund (Pat) Brown.

Years later, Reagan would insist that he was dragged into the race kicking and screaming, that he was not eager to make a huge change in his life. He was in his midfifties, and he and Nancy had a beautiful home in Pacific Palisades, and their social circle was based on Hollywood, not Sacramento. Reagan recalled telling would-be supporters that he had no interest in running for office, explaining, "I'm an actor, not a politician."

Behind the scenes, however, the actor was having serious political conversations with some of California's most prominent Republican contributors and fundraisers. He met with grass-roots Republican activists in his home to discuss state politics, a topic that was entirely new to him—The Speech, after all, was national in context, dealing with big issues that had little resonance in statewide elections. A growing number of Republican elected officials came to the conclusion, after hearing Reagan speak at party gatherings in early 1965, that he would be a strong candidate despite his lack of experience. In March of that year, several Republican organizations in the state either endorsed Reagan for governor or passed resolutions urging him to run.

He hated flying, but as a statewide candidate in California, he'd have no choice but to fly from engagement to engagement. After talking with supporters like Holmes Tuttle and Henry Salvatori, who had become millionaires despite very modest childhoods, Reagan agreed to barnstorm the state, speaking to community service groups rather than partisan Republican organizations. If all went well—if Reagan believed his message, the message contained in versions of The Speech, was well received—he would take the plunge.

On January 4, 1966, after long talks with Nancy and much soul-searching, Ronald Reagan announced his candidacy for governor of California.

Brown, a two-term incumbent, could not have been more relieved. He had survived a difficult reelection challenge in 1962, defeating Richard Nixon, a two-time vice president and the narrow loser of the 1960 presidential election. Nixon was a nationally known politician, a canny, tough opponent. Ronald Reagan was … an actor! If Brown could handle Nixon, surely he would make quick work of this novice who so recently costarred with a chimpanzee in the film *Bedtime for Bonzo*.

Then again, there were no guarantees that Reagan would actually be the Republican nominee. Before Reagan could challenge Brown, he would have to win his new party's nomination in a primary election against a former mayor of San Francisco, George Christopher. A professional politician, Christopher seemed to resent Reagan's audacity and inexperience. He attacked Reagan with such ferocity at a convention of black Republicans that Reagan actually stormed out of the hall, although he was later persuaded to return. "That day, I suppose, was all part of my political education," Reagan wrote later.[1]

More than tempers were flaring in California in 1966. Ronald Reagan's political debut took place against the backdrop of student unrest on the campuses of California's vaunted state university system and deadly riots in the Watts neighborhood of Los Angeles. Watts burned for six days in

August 1965, after a white police officer stopped a black motorist who was driving recklessly. In a scene that would be repeated, with local variations, in many American cities in the coming years, a confrontation between the police and local residents grew larger and angrier, leading to a full-scale riot. Thirty-four people died.

The year before, hundreds of students at the University of California at Berkeley had been arrested after taking over several buildings and threatening to shut down the entire campus. At issue was the university's prohibition against political activism on campus, which provoked confrontations between university officials and students from the new Free Speech Movement. Protests led to encounters with campus police; confrontations led to protracted disruptions; and finally Governor Brown ordered the state police to break up the standoff at Berkeley. Just as Watts was a foreshadowing of the strife that would consume many American cities in the late 1960s, the protests at Berkeley in late 1964 would be the first of many disturbing scenes on campuses throughout the nation.

Brown, who had given a speech in 1961 defending and even encouraging nonviolent student protests, hoped the arrests would put an end to the issue. But for another emerging political movement—this one centered in California's Orange County—Brown's actions were too little, too late. Tens of thousands of suburban homeowners saw the students not as principled radicals, but as spoiled kids who needed to be brought in line. They cheered when Reagan said that students in the state system were bound to follow the rules, or leave. State-subsidized higher education was not a right, Reagan argued, but a privilege, and students ought to conduct themselves accordingly.

In April 1966, Reagan chose a college campus setting for a major speech in the middle of his primary campaign against former Mayor Christopher. But the venue was not Berkeley or any of the other state universities, but the University of Southern California, a private school in Los Angeles known for its conservative student body and faculty. At USC, the neophyte candidate faced a friendly audience, the kind he would not have encountered had he spoken at one of California's nine state university campuses.

In his speech, Reagan outlined what he called "the creative society," deliberately drawing a contrast with President Lyndon Johnson's concept of a Great Society driven by new government programs and entitlements.

Although the speech contained several California-specific references—to the state's "skyrocketing crime rate" and its "unfriendly attitude toward business"—Reagan's main theme was national in scope, and, typically, it was about broad strokes rather than individual proposals.

It was not, in other words, the kind of stump speech voters often heard in elections for state offices. But then again, Reagan was unlike any other recent candidate for statewide office in California—although not because he was an actor. California sent onetime Broadway star Helen Gahagan Douglas to the House of Representatives from 1944 to 1950, when she lost a U.S. Senate race to a young up-and-comer named Richard Nixon. And in 1965, Reagan's friend George Murphy, a Hollywood song and dance man, was elected to the Senate. Indeed, the prominence of actors in California politics inspired satirical balladeer Tom Lehrer to write:

> Hollywood's often tried to mix
> Show business with politics.
> From Helen Gahagan
> To ... Ronald Reagan?

What distinguished Reagan, then, was not his show-business pedigree, but his ideological politics, his ability to explain his ideas to a mass audience, and his harsh critique of the Republican Party's moderate eastern establishment. Less than two years removed from Barry Goldwater's disastrous presidential campaign, Reagan eagerly embraced ideas that voters seemingly had rejected, loudly and clearly.

Reagan opened his speech with a nod to the fresh young faces in front of him. There was a time, he said, when he was one of them, and like them, he once questioned the values and authority of his elders. He didn't blame them, because he found fault with the older generation, too. "We are confused and we have confused you with a double standard of morality," he said, immediately signaling that this speech would hardly be a nuts-and-bolts monologue about, say, state highway funding. Because people accepted "double-dealing at government levels," Americans had "lost our capacity to get angry when decisions are not based on moral truth, but on political expediency."

If Californians were not used to this kind of talk from politicians, Reagan was glad to tell them why. "To begin with—I am not a politician," he said. "I am an ordinary citizen with a deep-seated belief that much of what troubles us has been brought about by politicians, and it's high time that more ordinary citizens brought the fresh air of common-sense thinking to bear on these problems." Reagan's audience at USC received a sneak preview of a theme that Reagan would revisit time and again over the next two decades and more. Even as governor of the nation's most populous state, even as president of the United States and leader of the Free World, Ronald Reagan presented himself as something other than a politician. As president, Reagan would seek to align himself with the ordinary American who viewed politics with suspicion, if not contempt—and there were a lot of those in the 1970s, in the aftermath of Watergate. But Reagan exploited the public's disgust with politics and politicians long before burglars were dispatched to the Watergate hotel in 1972. He became a latter-day populist, but with an ideological twist: rather than campaign against big business, as the populists of the late 19th century did, Reagan campaigned against big government and the power relationships of the 1960s.

Ironically, Reagan's message was not so far removed from those put forward on other campuses throughout California. There, too, politicians were blamed and scorned for all that seemed wrong about America. Students were trying to wrangle power away from those who had it. So, in his own way, was Ronald Reagan, albeit with a vastly different purpose in mind.

Moving to his ultimate target, the fledgling Great Society, Reagan said that it was no longer enough to look to the federal government for solutions. "The trouble with that solution," he said, "is that for every ounce of federal help we get, we surrender an ounce of personal freedom. The Great Society grows greater every day—greater in cost, greater in inefficiency and greater in waste."

What to do? Reagan conceded that President Johnson's Great Society programs were framed by what he called "humanitarian goals," and even suggested that the programs might "achieve those goals." He wondered, though, if such programs were the best way "of achieving those goals."

"What is obviously needed is not more government, but better government, seeking a solution to the problems that will not add to bureaucracy, or unbalance the budget, or further centralize power," he said. "Therefore,

I propose a constructive alternative to the Great Society, which I have chosen to call 'A Creative Society.' While leadership and initiative for this Creative Society should begin in the governor's office, it would be the task of the entire state government to discover, enlist and mobilize the incredibly rich human resources of California, calling on the best in every field to revise and review our government structure and present plans for streamlining it and making it more efficient and more effective."

Many of the themes and techniques of Reagan's later speeches—the tales of uplift, the homage to the American spirit, and the frequently unverifiable anecdote used to illustrate a policy goal—were very much on display in the USC speech. He told his audience about a "businessman in Texas brought up in poverty" who founded a ranch that offered an alterative to crime for three hundred boys a year. He said there was "no problem that cannot be resolved" thanks to "the tremendous potential of our people." And he said that he had "been told there is work in our public institutions, some of which could be performed by unemployables, even illiterates, enough to give jobs to 50,000."

This was just the sort of anecdote that would enrage Reagan's critics through the years. He had been told: by whom? Had he checked the veracity of this story? Where did he get the figure of 50,000 jobs? Critics, however, missed Reagan's point. The details didn't matter, in the end. The larger argument was more important, because it struck a chord. If Reagan's anecdotes didn't sound true—regardless of their veracity—they would not have had staying power. Reagan touched a nerve among some Californians who believed that, in words Reagan would later use, government was the problem, not business, and certainly not the character of the American people.

The Creative Society, in Reagan's view, would be a partnership between the dynamism of individuals and necessary oversight of government. California's welfare program, "which doubled in the last five years," ought to be examined by "campus researchers and others experienced in philanthropy and public service." The Creative Society would look to "the best brains of industry and the community" to make California more attractive to business.

"The Creative Society, in other words, is simply a return to the people of the privilege of self-government," he said.

In asserting that government had grown distant from the people it was designed to serve, Reagan had struck populist gold. Pat Brown had no idea what was about to hit him.

Reagan won in his first bid for elective office, taking nearly 60 percent of the vote.

Ronald Reagan being sworn in as Governor of California by Associate Justice Marshall McComb at the State Capitol in Sacramento

Ronald Reagan takes a break on the 1976 presidential campaign trail at a winter resort in Dixville Notch, New Hampshire

CHAPTER 3

We Carry the Message

Speech to the 1976
Republican National Convention
August 19, 1976

TRACK 3

RONALD REAGAN'S TWO TERMS AS GOVERNOR OF CALIFORNIA WERE tumultuous, not surprising given the times. His tenure coincided with eight of the most contentious years in American history. When he took office on January 1, 1967, the war in Vietnam was controversial but not yet explosive, the nation's cities seemed at peace, Martin Luther King Jr. and Robert F. Kennedy were very much alive, and the postwar political consensus seemed intact. By the time he left office at the end of 1974, the war had inspired a virtual rebellion among young people, riots had turned large swaths of America's cities into rubble, King and Kennedy were dead by assassins' bullets, and the Watergate scandal had driven Richard Nixon from the presidency.

Reagan still was a popular man when he left Sacramento, no small accomplishment in an age of disillusion with politics and government. He was a complete neophyte in 1967, but contrary to expectations, he showed a capacity and willingness to learn how government works, how deals are cut, and how policy is decided. He spoke as an ideologue, but he governed as a principled pragmatist. He and the Democrats who ran California's legislature agreed on a welfare reform package that reduced the number of people in the system (from about 1.6 million to 1.3 million) and emphasized job training. He also dramatically increased spending for education—it nearly doubled during his two terms—and oversaw implementation of expensive new programs like special education. Property taxpayers saw some relief, thanks in part to Reagan's emphasis on controlling government costs.

Reagan promised voters he would serve no more than two terms, and he was as good as his word. His timing could not have been better. Nixon resigned in August 1974, and when voters went to the polls three months later, they punished Republicans throughout the country. Reagan's popularity was not enough to prevent a Democratic victory in the race to succeed him as governor. In fact, the winning candidate was none other than Edmund G. Brown Jr., better known as Jerry, and better known still as the son of the man Reagan defeated in 1966.

The citizen-politician who went to Sacramento in 1967 was now a seasoned politico whose ambitions were far from satisfied. The presidential election of 1976 had figured to offer Reagan a golden opportunity, but Nixon's resignation changed the dynamics of national politics. Nixon's successor, Gerald Ford, would be eligible to run for a full term of his own—had Nixon not resigned, he would have been a lame duck that year, allowing for a wide-open competition among Republicans. If Reagan wanted to run for president in 1976, he would have to challenge an incumbent from his own party. No Republican of stature had been so bold since Theodore Roosevelt challenged William Howard Taft's renomination in 1912.

Ford was a genial, well-liked man who represented a solidly centrist middle ground in the Republican Party. What's more, as president, he had power to dispense to friends and allies; and as a veteran of Capitol Hill, he had no shortage of chits to call in. More than anything else, though, he made a poor villain. A populist insurgency often requires a villain who personifies all that the insurgents loathe, but Ford simply seemed too decent and dependable for that role. He was not Nelson Rockefeller, the former governor of New York who did, in fact, play the role of liberal villain for Republican dissenters on the right.

But when Ford succeeded Nixon and promptly nominated Rockefeller as his vice president, Reagan and his allies took notice. The Ford administration would bear watching.

Although Ford's popularity and reputation took a hit when he pardoned Nixon a month after taking office, Reagan's concerns had nothing to do with the pardon and its repercussions. He saw Ford as a creature of Washington who represented not change, but the status quo. As he contemplated the future, he continued to give speeches to like-minded conservative groups. In one of them, he proposed a wholesale transfer of federal programs—for welfare, education, housing, health care, and other initiatives—to the states.

It was becoming clear that Ronald Reagan had something on his mind, and on November 20, 1975, he made it official: he announced that he would challenge Gerald Ford for the 1976 presidential nomination. The Republican Party, so badly bloodied in the aftermath of Watergate, now faced the certainty of civil war. At about the same time, Rockefeller announced that he would not be a candidate for vice president in 1976, a move that allowed Ford room to maneuver as he tried to appease the party's right wing.

Reagan almost immediately became the front-runner in the crucial New Hampshire primary, where his antitax message resonated. A Reagan victory there would mean a quick end to the party's rare internecine battle, as a defeated Ford would have been hard-pressed to continue. Precedent was on Reagan's side: Lyndon Johnson dropped his reelection bid in 1968 when his margin of victory over insurgent Eugene McCarthy was considered too small (Johnson won 49.6 percent to McCarthy's 41.4 percent), and Harry Truman announced that he would not seek another term in 1952 after he lost to Estes Kefauver in that year's primary in the Granite State.

But a hard-charging Ford caught up with Reagan in the days leading up to the primary, earning the president a narrow victory. That set the stage for a prolonged, bitter, and divisive battle through the winter and spring of 1976. Reagan found traction with his criticism of Ford's foreign policy, which he denounced as insufficiently tough on the Soviet Union. He also struck a chord when he argued against the Ford administration's preliminary talks with Panama over the future of the U.S.-run Panama Canal. The waterway, Reagan said, was a strategic asset that ought to remain in U.S. hands.

The candidates battled through the spring, as momentum swung back and forth, leading to the final set of primaries in early June. After Reagan claimed victory in his home state of California, and Ford finished first in Ohio and New Jersey, neither man had enough delegates to guarantee a first-ballot victory at the Republican National Convention in August. Slightly more than a hundred delegates were not committed to either candidate, although many were expected to side with the incumbent. In an effort to win over uncommitted delegates worried that Reagan was too far to the right, the challenger announced that he would name Pennsylvania Senator Richard Schweiker, a moderate to liberal lawmaker, as his vice president if he won the nomination.

Some of Reagan's staunchest supporters were aghast. Senator Jesse Helms of North Carolina talked openly about abandoning Reagan. As the convention opened in Kansas City, Missouri, Reagan's allies pressed for a vote on a rule that would have forced Ford to announce his choice for vice president before the delegates cast their presidential votes. If Ford were forced to show his hand, Reagan's people believed, his choice might alienate some delegates. But the tactic failed. Reagan was doomed.

The roll call of the states began on the night of August 18, and it spilled past midnight. Finally, when West Virginia, one of the last states to be called, cast its votes for Ford, the incumbent clinched the nomination. A victorious Ford paid a courtesy call to Reagan's hotel room, a magnanimous gesture but one that did not heal the hard feelings between the two men. They fought each other in an epic political battle, and it ended in the worst possible way. The party was bitterly and almost evenly divided at a time when it would need every bit of energy and determination to retain its hold on the White House. The first presidential election since Nixon's resignation figured to be difficult enough for Republicans, but the Ford–Reagan contest made the party's task that much more difficult.

On the night of August 19, Gerald Ford delivered his acceptance speech to the divided convention. When it was over, the nominee was joined by his wife, Betty, his choice for vice president, Senator Bob Dole of Kansas, the incumbent vice president, Rockefeller, and his wife, Happy. Music played as the politicians and their spouses waved to the delegates, nearly half of whom were Reagan supporters.

Reagan and his wife Nancy were in the hall, watching from their box. Ford, in his moment of victory, looked up to the Reagans, pointed them out, and asked them to join the victory party. Television cameras captured the drama as Reagan demurred, waving off the gesture. But Ford persisted, and the Reagans left their seats to make the short journey to the convention stage.

It was, under any circumstances, a remarkable scene: Reagan, it seemed, inspired more cheers, certainly louder cheers, than Ford did. Then Ford invited Reagan to step to the podium to say a few words, a generous gesture considering the antipathy between the two men. With Nancy, dressed in white, on his right, and the president and vice president hovering over his left shoulder, Reagan addressed the more than two thousand delegates and millions watching on television.

As he gathered his thoughts, Reagan first thanked Ford for his warm greeting of Nancy, which, he said, "filled my heart with joy." He then launched into a personal anecdote, as he often did, to make a point not about his duel with Ford or about the coming general election, but about nothing less than freedom, and the threat of nuclear war.

"I had an assignment the other day," he told the delegates and those watching on television. "Someone asked me to write a letter for a time capsule that is going to be opened in Los Angeles a hundred years from now, on our Tricentennial." It seemed, he said, like an easy assignment: he'd write about some of the issues he cared about. As he thought about the task, and as he looked out onto "the blue Pacific" and "the Santa Ynez Mountains" during a car ride, he wrestled with what he might say about "a world in which the great powers have poised and aimed at each other horrible missiles of destruction …

"And suddenly it dawned on me, those who would read this letter a hundred years from now will know whether those missiles were fired. They will now whether we met our challenge: Whether they have the freedoms that we have known up until now will depend on what we do here."

This, he said, was not a moment to shirk responsibility. Reagan's was a Cold War message delivered during a time of détente with the Soviet Union, a détente he believed was working to the Soviets' advantage. The United States, he implied, sought accommodation at a time when it ought to be speaking out on behalf of freedom.

Of his future readers, he asked: "Will they look back with appreciation and say, 'Thank God for those people in 1976 who headed off that loss of freedom, who kept us now 100 years later free, who kept out world from nuclear destruction?'

"And if we failed, they probably won't get to read the letter at all because it spoke of individual freedom, and they won't be allowed to talk of that or read of it."

It was a stark and sobering message, delivered at a moment of celebration. But if Reagan seemed determined to cast a shadow on Gerald

Ford's victory party, his listeners did not seem to mind. They listened, silently, enraptured—and thinking, perhaps, that they had nominated the wrong man.

"This is our challenge," he said, "and this is why ... we have got to quit talking to each other and about each other and go and communicate to the world that we may be fewer in numbers than we have ever been, but we carry the message they are waiting for."

This was his pep talk, his message to Republicans battered by Watergate, that they might be bloodied, but they were on the right side of history, and ought to act accordingly. It was also an attempt to put aside the bitterness that he helped stir up with his dramatic and determined challenge of a sitting president and fellow Republican.

"We must go forth here united, determined that what a great general said a few years ago is true: 'There is no substitute for victory, Mr. President.'"

With that citation of General Douglas MacArthur's famous maxim, the hall exploded. The cheers took some of the sting out of Reagan's jab, for implicit in his words was the suggestion that Gerald Ford might be willing to settle for something less than victory. That, indeed, was Reagan's complaint with the Nixon-Ford-Kissinger policy of détente in the first place.

They were united on stage: Ford and Reagan, Rockefeller and Dole, and their wives. But the party's wounds, the fresh ones from 1976 as well as those still bleeding from the wars of Watergate, were not so easily healed. The party limped out of Kansas City with Ford well behind in the polls.

The incumbent battled back against the Democratic nominee, Jimmy Carter, but in the end, Ford was defeated. Carter took just over half the vote in an extremely close election.

But in defeat, the Republican Party knew that it had a star in the wings: Ronald Reagan.

Gerald Ford thanks Ronald Reagan for his remarks during the 1976 Republican national convention in Kansas City, Missouri

Ronald Reagan delivers his acceptance speech at the Republican national convention

CHAPTER 4

Renewing the American Compact

Acceptance Speech at the
Republican National Convention
July 17, 1980

TRACK 4

ONALD REAGAN SPENT THE CARTER YEARS DELIVERING SPEECHES AROUND
the country, just as he had traveled California in the months leading
up to the 1966 gubernatorial campaign. He had his own political
action committee, Citizens for the Republic, and he leaped at opportunities
to keep his name and his voice before the American people. After Jimmy
Carter signed a treaty with Panama relinquishing U.S. control over the
Canal Zone in late 1977, Reagan sparred with fellow conservative William
F. Buckley in a memorable, nationally televised debate over the treaty.
Reagan argued that the United States should maintain its control over the
canal, that access to the waterway was necessary for America's role as a
global power. The Senate approved the treaty by a single vote in April
1978, but Reagan's advocacy was not in vain: he further endeared himself
to conservative Republicans, and he continued to keep his name in the
presidential mix.

The late 1970s were difficult times for the United States. The Carter
administration grappled without much success against high unemployment,
high interest rates, and high inflation—a politically volatile combination.
Stagflation, it came to be called—a combination of stagnant economic
growth and rampant inflation. By the middle of Carter's term, inflation

reached 12 percent, and unemployment hovered at around 7 percent. Interest rates were just below 12 percent, and would skyrocket to more than 21 percent within two years.

Adding to the nation's burdens was an energy shortage brought on when oil-exporting countries sharply reduced supplies. Carter asked Americans to turn down their thermostats, drive less frequently, and otherwise conserve energy. He also declared that the country was suffering from a collective crisis of confidence, although he certainly did little to ease that crisis when he asked for the mass resignation of his cabinet in 1979.

When Iranian students stormed the U.S. Embassy in Teheran and seized fifty-two Americans as hostages in November 1979, the crisis of confidence that Carter identified became even more acute. Washington was powerless as the hostage crisis was played out every night on television news shows, which showed the Iranian students openly taunting a wounded superpower. The Soviet Union invaded Afghanistan on December 25, adding to anxieties that the United States was a spent force abroad.

Carter's problems seemed to offer Republicans a golden opportunity to avenge their massive losses in 1974 and 1976, when Watergate was fresh in the minds of voters. Nine Republicans already were campaigning for the party's presidential nomination when the hostage crisis began. On November 13, 1979, a tenth candidate added his name to the field: Ronald Reagan.

His announcement took few by surprise, for Reagan's public profile in the years since his defeat in 1976 left little doubt that he intended to make another try for the White House. Even though he had broad name recognition and had come within a few dozen votes of defeating Ford, he was by no means considered a favorite for the nomination. He turned sixty-nine years old just before the New Hampshire primary in February, and while he was in superb health and certainly looked years younger, nobody his age had ever been elected president. For that matter, no divorced candidate had ever been elected, either.

The campaign's first test came in mid-January in the newly important Iowa party caucuses. Reagan led in precaucus polls, but former CIA Director George H.W. Bush outworked him, and finished first with 33 percent of the vote. Bush, scion of the Eastern Establishment Republicanism that Reagan disdained—his father was a senator from Connecticut—took his campaign to New Hampshire with a chance to finish off Reagan.

Although there were five other major candidates still in the Republican race, Bush and Reagan were at the head of the pack. Aides for the two fron-trunners agreed that the two men should debate each other face-to-face in a high school gym in Nashua, without the other candidates. The Bush campaign, however, refused to split the cost of the debate, so the Reagan campaign picked up the tab. It would prove to be a wise investment.

Hours before the debate, members of Reagan's campaign staff called the other Republican candidates, urging them to come to Nashua that evening because Reagan might be able to get them into the debate after all. Four of the excluded candidates—Senator Howard Baker of Tennessee, Senator Bob Dole of Kansas, and Congressmen John Anderson and Philip Crane, both of Illinois—seized what they saw as an opportunity for much-needed exposure, only to serve as unwitting foils for one of Ronald Reagan's memorable (and rare) displays of anger. Another candidate, John Connolly, was out of state and so was not a part of the drama.

When the candidates showed up at the gym, Reagan, who was unaware of his campaign's machinations until just before the event, met with them while members of his campaign staff met with the Bush camp. Reagan decided the other Republicans ought to participate, but the Bush camp refused to change the agreed-upon rules of engagement. As the parlay went on, Reagan abruptly walked out to the stage with the other candidates while Bush remained in his chair on stage, refusing to acknowledge the drama unfolding just a few feet away. The four other candidates stood behind Reagan, looking very serious and determined. The crowd loved the unscripted moment, and spectators cried out in favor of a free-for-all with all six candidates. Above the din, Reagan tried to explain to the debate's moderator, Jon Breen, editor of the *Nashua Telegraph*, why he thought the other candidates should be included. Breen ordered a technician to cut off Reagan's microphone. The genial, easygoing Ronald Reagan of stage and screen gave way to a Ronald Reagan rarely seen in public. "I paid for this microphone, Mr. Green," he said, calling the editor by the wrong name. The crowd roared in approval.[1]

Reagan won the New Hampshire primary, thanks in part to the public's approval of his defiant words in Nashua. He took 51 percent of the vote in the crowded field of seven, and he never looked back. Reagan won twenty-nine (of thirty-three) primaries, and while Bush battled doggedly through the spring, he gave up in mid-May. The nomination was Reagan's. The sixty-nine-year-old man finished first in a political marathon.

A revived and optimistic Republican Party gathered in Detroit in mid-July to ratify Reagan's victory and proclaim him as the party's nominee. These were formalities, but there remained a bit of important, but unfinished, business: the selection of a vice president.

As the convention got underway on July 14, former President Gerald Ford delivered a fire-breathing denunciation of the Carter administration and an enthusiastic endorsement of Reagan's candidacy. That speech led to an idea in the Reagan camp: what if Ford, a tireless campaigner who almost beat Carter four years earlier, would consider the vice presidency? Reagan aides sent out feelers to Ford's aides, leading to a flurry of secret meetings and discussions. As a former president, what sort of role would Ford have in a Reagan administration? Would Ford, a veteran of Washington, overshadow the newcomer, Reagan? What would the party's newly energized right wing think of Ford, who represented the discredited Republican center?

The discussions reached a stalemate, but Ford put an end to any further talks by taking himself out of the running. While delegates listened to speeches in Joe Louis Arena, Ford called on Reagan in his suite to tell him that he no longer wished to be considered for vice president. The tensions between the two men vanished as the former president gave the future president a hug and promised to work on his behalf. When Ford left, Reagan breathed a sigh of relief and said, "I think we're friends now."[2]

The Reagan team turned to George Bush, another old Washington hand and seemingly a symbol of the centrist politics Reagan and his followers opposed. But Bush had proven to be a worthy, determined opponent during the primary season. Reagan admired his tenacity. The deal was done.

On the night of July 17, 1980, Ronald Reagan took center stage to accept his party's nomination for president. The last time he addressed his party, it was divided and dispirited despite the flag-waving and cheering. This time, the Republicans were united, enthusiastic, and, perhaps most important, they could taste victory.

As Reagan basked in the delegates' cheers, a delegate to his right held up a handmade sign that read "Surfers for Reagan." The floor was a sea of hastily made Reagan-Bush placards. The nominee, in a dark suit, his hair slicked back and glistening in the hall's lights, stood above rows of red and blue carnations lining the stage.

The moment was one of triumph. The message, however, was stern and unvarnished. America, Reagan said, faced "three grave threats to our very existence, any one of which could destroy us. We face a disintegrating economy, a weakened defense, and an energy policy based on the sharing of scarcity."

Reagan was never shy about conjuring images of national catastrophe. They were embedded in his GE speech and other rhetoric from his days as a politician in training. In 1980, however, the possibility of national decline seemed all too real, so Reagan's stark warning did not seem as out of place as it might have a decade earlier.

There was another threat, too, and this one was not as quantifiable as the price of oil or the number of combat-ready troops. Like Carter, Reagan saw a crisis of spirit in the country. But unlike Carter, Reagan placed the crisis not among the people, but among politicians. "The major issue of this campaign is the direct political, personal, and moral responsibility of Democratic Party leadership—in the White House and in Congress—for this unprecedented calamity which has befallen us." The words were harsh, and so was his tone. He believed the nation was headed in the wrong direction. Of the Democratic leaders, he said, "They say that the United States has had its day in the sun; that our nation has passed its zenith. They expect you to tell your children that the American people no longer have the will to cope with their problems; that the future will be one of sacrifice and few opportunities." With a pause for emphasis, he added: "My fellow citizens, I utterly reject that view."

With those words, Reagan established the theme of the coming campaign: President Carter represented the party of decline, and he and the Republicans represented hope. And hope, he believed, always defeated despair.

"My view of government places trust not in one person or one party, but in those values that transcend persons and parties," he said, taking a jab at Carter's pledge in 1976 that Americans could trust him after the embarrassments of Watergate. "The trust is where it belongs—in the people. The responsibility to live up to that trust is where it belongs, in their elected leaders. That kind of relationship, between the people and their elected leaders, is a special kind of compact." Reagan proposed to renew the idea of an American compact, which he traced back to the *Mayflower*. "Isn't it once again time to renew our compact of freedom; to pledge to each other all that is best in our lives; all that gives meaning to them—for the sake of this, our beloved and blessed land?"

The delegates applauded in agreement. Reagan's acceptance speech was not just a laundry list of promises, a dull white paper of policy proposals. It was a soaring call to revive the nation's fortunes, a task that could only be achieved by the people, not by government. It was quite unlike any speech given in the recent, dreary past.

It was that dreariness that Reagan attacked: "Our problems are both acute and chronic, yet all we hear from those in positions of leadership are the same tired proposals for more government tinkering, more meddling and more control—all of which led us to this state in the first place. Can anyone look at the record of this administration and say, 'Well done?'"

This was impassioned rhetoric for sure, but Reagan was careful to avoid sounding impassioned. Americans were hearing him for the first time as a presidential nominee; he did not want them to conclude that he was too unreliable, too ideological, for the presidency, as his critics suggested.

Even still, many of his proposals had an ideological edge to them. His listeners in the convention hall, the new faces of a new Republican Party, roared when they heard Reagan demanding a substantial reduction of the federal government and a 30-percent reduction in income taxes. These were the voices that cheered antitax revolts in California and elsewhere, and now they had one of their own running for president.

In discussing the nation's place in the world, Reagan summed up the country's mood in a sentence: "Who does not feel rising alarm when the question in any discussion of foreign policy is no longer, 'Should we do something?' but 'Do we have the capacity to do anything?'" In a foreshadowing of an argument he would make to great effect later in the campaign, Reagan said: "No American should vote until he or she has asked: Is the United States stronger and more respected than it was three and a half years ago? Is the world today a safer place to live?" Shouts of "No!" from the convention floor provided the answer.

The speech, however, would not and could not be a litany of complaint and criticism. Reagan's optimism would be one of his campaign's most important virtues, and despite the gloomy picture he painted of

America in 1980, he made it clear that he did not consider hard times to be permanent. He quoted his favorite early American author, Tom Paine, who said, "We have it on our power to begin the world over again." Then, as he had in his televised address in October 1964, he quoted from his onetime idol, Franklin D. Roosevelt, who inspired Americans during the depths of the Depression.

"I believe that this generation of Americans today has a rendezvous with destiny," Reagan said. "The American spirit is ... ready to blaze into life if you and I are willing to do what has to be done; the practical, down-to-earth things that will stimulate our economy, increase productivity, and put America back to work ... The time is now, my fellow Americans, to recapture our destiny, to take it into our own hands."

He closed by asking the delegates to join him in a silent prayer. They did, and then exploded in cheers.

Ronald Reagan and Jimmy Carter shake hands at the presidential debate in Cleveland, Ohio

CHAPTER 5

Are You Better Off?

Debate with President Jimmy Carter
October 28, 1980

TRACK 5

T HE MODERN TRADITION OF PRESIDENTIAL DEBATES WAS VERY MUCH A WORK
in progress in 1980. It was not taken for granted, as it would be in
later elections, that the two main candidates would meet face-to-
face in what amounted to more of a joint press conference than an actual,
freewheeling debate. The famed televised debates between John Kennedy
and Richard Nixon in 1960 did not establish a precedent—there were no
debates in 1964, '68, or '72. When Gerald Ford agreed to debate challenger
Jimmy Carter in 1976, it marked the first time in U.S. history that a sitting
president deigned to debate the issues with an opponent during an election
campaign.

Both the Carter and Reagan camps discussed the possibility of debates
during the summer of 1980, but there was a stumbling block in the independent candidacy of Illinois Congressman John Anderson. Polls showed
that while Anderson was a Republican, he was taking votes away from
Carter, not from his fellow Republican, Reagan. Anderson seemed to offer
an alternative for voters who opposed Carter but could not bring themselves to vote for Reagan.

Reagan was eager to debate the president because he believed he had the
issues on his side. But Carter and his camp wanted no part of a three-person

debate with Anderson and Reagan, fearing the lift it would give Anderson in states where Carter needed every vote he could get. Reagan and Anderson went on without him, meeting for a debate on September 21 in Baltimore. It was not especially riveting, but it proved to be a useful exercise for Reagan, who avoided mistakes and otherwise kept pace with Anderson, who was articulate and bright, if somehow preachy and self-righteous.

Carter's absence was noted and criticized in print coverage of the debate. While the president was under no obligation to participate, he looked like a man who had something to hide. Within a few weeks, the Reagan and Carter camps announced that the two main contenders would meet face-to-face after all, on October 28 in the Convention Center Music Hall in Cleveland, Ohio. The debate figured to be a pivotal moment in the campaign, coming a week before Election Day.

Although Reagan entered the fall campaign with momentum and had shown during the primary season that he was a superb campaigner, the weeks between the convention and his debate date with Carter were not without stumbles. Two of them involved the tripwire of race. On August 3, Reagan traveled to Philadelphia, Mississippi, to speak at the Neshoba County Fair. His words on that hot summer day were about states' rights, a racially loaded term that many whites used to defend the South's segregationist past. Reagan promised that he would return to the states the powers that the federal government had taken away from them, although he did not point out that many Southern states abused their powers to enforce segregation. Not far from the fairgrounds, in 1964, three civil rights workers were brutally murdered in one of era's most infamous crimes. Reagan's presence there, and his invocation of states' rights with all of its implications about race and white supremacy, led to passionate criticism and doubts about his judgment.

A few weeks later, during a whirlwind tour of industrial states, Reagan noted that while he was in the North, Carter was speaking in the town of Tuscumbia, Alabama, which Reagan described as "the city that gave birth to and is the parent body of the Ku Klux Klan." It was an outrageous outburst, and Reagan knew it. "I blew it," he admitted. "I just should have never said what I said." It was not just a cheap shot—it was just plain wrong: while there were Klan elements in Tuscumbia, it was hardly a center of Klan activity. Reagan had to apologize. His campaign, his credibility, and his fitness for office once again came under question.[1]

As the debate with Carter grew near, Reagan submitted to a mock grilling from supporters like future U.N. Ambassador Jeanne Kirkpatrick and journalist George Will. David Stockman, a young assistant, played the role of Carter in the rehearsals, reprising the role he had played as Anderson in preparation for the previous debate.

While Reagan and his team went over their issues and answers, they feared that all their preparation might be in vain. While Reagan led in nationwide polls in late October, his strategists were concerned that Carter might yet find a way to win release of the American hostages in Iran. Such an "October surprise," as it was called, certainly would move wavering voters to Carter's column and perhaps inspire a wholesale defection from Reagan's camp. Fear of the unknown gave special urgency to Reagan's debate preparations. A bad performance, combined with an October surprise, would give Carter momentum at precisely the wrong time.

The two men strode onstage in Cleveland to face a panel of four journalists: Marvin Stone of *U.S. News & World Report*, Harris Ellis of the *Christian Science Monitor*, William Hilliard of the Portland *Oregonian*, and Barbara Walters of *ABC News*. Both candidates wore dark business suits; a hint of a white handkerchief peeked out from the left breast pocket of Reagan's jacket. Carter's podium was on the left side of the television screen, Reagan on the right. Behind them were television-friendly blue drapes.

Anticipating, correctly, that Carter would be on the offensive, Reagan seized the initiative in the debate's opening minutes when he was asked about his differences with Carter over the use of American military power. "I don't know what the differences might be," Reagan said, "because I don't know what Mr. Carter's policies are. I do know what he has said about mine." One of Reagan's many gifts as a communicator was his ability to convey passion and even annoyance in a gentle, soft voice. He did so in this debate from the outset, knowing that Carter would try to portray him as a dangerous ideologue.

The issue of American power, in fact, cut to the heart of the Democratic criticism of Reagan: that he would be a trigger-happy commander in chief who would shoot first and ask questions later—like a cowboy in one of the Westerns he starred in during his Hollywood years. Reagan tried to diffuse that issue in his first answer. "I'm a father of sons," he said. "I have a grandson. I don't ever want to see another generation of young Americans bleed their lives into sandy beachheads in the Pacific, or rice paddies and jungles in … Asia or the muddy battlefields of Europe."

Despite that argument, Carter did try to portray Reagan as a knee-jerk anti-Communist who would embrace confrontation at the expense of negotiation. He attacked Reagan's position against a proposed Strategic Arms Limitation Treaty (SALT II), and charged that Reagan would insist on American nuclear superiority before entering into any negotiations with the Soviets. "This would mean the resumption of a very dangerous nuclear arms race," Carter said.

Put on the defensive, Reagan said that he supported mutual reductions in nuclear arms and would not insist on American superiority. Under the debate's rules, Carter was allowed to respond to Reagan's reply. "I think, to close out this discussion, it would be better to put into perspective what we're talking about," Carter said. "I had a discussion with my daughter, Amy, the other day, before I came here, to ask her what the most important issue was. She said she thought nuclear weaponry—and the control of nuclear arms."

Carter was attempting to put a human face, the face of a thirteen-year-old girl, on an issue that seemed abstract—negotiations about weapons that were hidden out of sight. But his answer was widely ridiculed, for it seemed as though he was taking his policy cues from a thirteen-year-old child.

Later on, when the debate moved to domestic issues, Carter attacked Reagan on Social Security and Medicare, suggesting that neither government program was safe in the hands of a conservative ideologue. These were familiar attacks, and Reagan, after his intense preparations and after a long campaign, surely knew they were coming.

Carter said that Reagan had begun "his political career campaigning around this nation against Medicare," and that he would stand in the way of further progress "toward national health insurance."

The debate's moderator, *ABC News* anchor Howard K. Smith, called on Reagan to respond.

Reagan looked to his right, towards Carter, and said, "There you go again." The four words came to him during his mock debate sessions, and he saved them for a moment of dramatic exasperation. It was an effective, homespun parry of Carter's line of attack. He went on to say that he opposed one version of Medicare legislation but supported another that, he said, would have provided better care for seniors. But the details of his reply were lost in the reaction to his opening line. There you go again.

After a discussion of women's issues, during which Reagan defended his opposition to the Equal Rights Amendment, the two candidates were invited to deliver short closing statements. Carter emphasized the loneliness of his job, perhaps to further drive home the point that Reagan could not be trusted with the heavy responsibilities of office. The "future of the nation—war, peace, involvement, reticence, thoughtfulness, care, consideration, concern—has to be made by the man in the Oval Office," he said. In trying to describe his fitness for office, and Reagan's unfitness, Carter managed to paint a dreary picture of politics, government, and the presidency.

When his turn came, Reagan turned the conversation outward. He would offer no homilies about the burdens of power. Instead, he turned to the burdens of those watching the debate on television.

"Next Tuesday," he said, "all of you will go to the polls, will stand there in the polling place and make a decision. I think when you make that decision, it might be well if you would ask yourself, are you better off than you were four years ago? Is it easier for you to go and buy things in the stores than it was four years ago? Is there more or less unemployment in the country than there was four years ago? Is America as respected throughout the world as it was? Do you feel our security is as safe, that we're as strong as we were four years ago? And if you answer all of those questions, yes, why then, I think your choice is very obvious as to whom you will vote for.

"If you don't agree, if you don't think that this course that we've been on for the last four years is what you would like to see us follow for the next four, then I could suggest another choice that you have."

Reagan conceded that he did not have the president's experience as a national leader, but as governor of California, he knew something about decision making. And he also knew why he wanted to take on new burdens—he wished to relieve the American people of some of theirs. He said he wanted to lead a "crusade" to "take government off the backs of the great people of this country, and turn you loose again to do those things that I know you can do so well, because you did them and made this country great."

A week later, the American people gave Ronald Reagan a smashing victory. Although the three-way nature of the race kept his percentage of the popular vote relatively low, just over half, he won 489 electoral votes to Carter's 44.

The burdens of power were now his.

PART TWO:

The First Term

1981–85

Ronald Reagan and Tip O'Neill in the Oval Office

Introduction

THE ECONOMY WAS RONALD REAGAN'S TOP PRIORITY UPON TAKING OFFICE, and he was prepared to move quickly to implement the tax cuts he promised as a candidate. Standing in his way was the formidable figure of Thomas P. (Tip) O'Neill of Massachusetts, Speaker of the heavily Democratic House of Representatives. While Reagan had a mandate for change, he would have to persuade large numbers of House Democrats to go along with his program.

The stage was set for a political brawl, but the dynamics changed drastically on March 30, when the president was seriously wounded by would-be assassin John Hinckley Jr. after a speech in Washington DC. Reagan's courage during the ordeal, his ability to crack a joke to his doctors before undergoing life-saving surgery, transformed him into not just a chief executive, but an American hero. When he addressed a joint session of Congress on April 28 after a month's recuperation, Democrats, Republicans, and the public cheered. Few presidents have ever had more political capital than Ronald Reagan did in the spring of 1981. And he used it to pass a budget that included a 25 percent reduction in taxes and a package of spending cuts to domestic programs.

The economy, however, did not respond as Reagan promised it would. The nation slid into a deep recession, putting tens of thousands out of work. Joining the displaced workers on the unemployment line were the nation's air traffic controllers, whom the president fired en masse when they went on strike on August 3.

Abroad, Reagan made it clear that the era of détente with the Soviet Union was over. In a speech in Great Britain in 1982, he predicted that Communism was headed for history's scrap heap. He upped the rhetorical ante the following year, publicly denouncing the Soviet Union as an "evil empire." But Reagan's policy consisted of more than words: in the face of massive protests, he deployed intermediate nuclear weapons in Europe to counter a previous Soviet deployment. The missiles were part of a huge military buildup that contributed to record-breaking deficits despite Reagan's support of a balanced budget.

Reagan and his aides saw Soviet handiwork in Central America, and so embarked on a policy of confrontation with the leftist Sandinista regime in Nicaragua while propping up a right-wing authoritarian government in El Salvador against a leftist rebellion.

Reagan's popularity fell as the recession of 1981–82 deepened. But by early 1983, there were signs of recovery, and the president's approval ratings began moving north. He began to turn his attention to more cosmic matters, proposing a missile defense system that, he said, could reduce the threat of nuclear war. Later in the year, as the Middle East erupted in violence, a suicide bomber attacked U.S. Marines deployed in Lebanon on a peacekeeping mission, killing 241. Within a matter of hours after the attack, U.S. forces invaded the island nation of Grenada in the Caribbean after the government was overthrown and U.S. students at a medical school seemed to be in danger.

The nation's mood was brighter as the election year of 1984 opened. Unemployment was down to less than 8 percent after hitting double digits. Inflation and interest rates were reduced dramatically. But the government was spending money it didn't have—the federal deficit approached $200 million. Critics worried about the red ink, but the public seemed less concerned. Reagan was as popular as ever as his reelection campaign began. A stirring speech in Normandy, France, to mark the fortieth anniversary of D-Day reminded critics and supporters alike that few politicians understood the art of communication better than Ronald Reagan.

Reagan stumbled in the home stretch of the fall campaign during the first of two debates with his challenger, former Vice President Walter

Mondale. Under a surprisingly aggressive attack from the ordinarily mild-mannered Mondale, Reagan seemed befuddled and confused. Questions about his age abounded, but when the two met again, Reagan's witty retort that he would not use his opponent's youth against him eased the nation's fears. Reagan won a smashing reelection in November, taking every state except Massachusetts and the District of Columbia. The election of 1984 solidified the Reagan Revolution and moved his party and the nation itself to the right.

The Reagans wave to crowds during Ronald Reagan's first inaugural parade

CHAPTER 6

A New Beginning

Ronald Reagan's First Inaugural Address
January 20, 1981

TRACK 6

NTIL RONALD REAGAN ARRIVED IN WASHINGTON DC, PRESIDENTIAL inaugurations were held on the east side of the Capitol—that is, the side that does not face the grassy expanse of the Mall and its iconic memorials. The new president and his team, masters of the language of image and symbols, signaled a new beginning by switching the inauguration ceremony from the nondescript east steps of the Capitol to the visually rich west.

The change was not just about pretty pictures. It was designed to provoke thought and reflection at a time when the nation seemed to have lost its way. In the narrative that Ronald Reagan embraced and personified, Americans have always looked to the west as a place of new beginnings and fresh starts. Reagan himself went west as a young man to seek his fortune, setting out on a journey that would, incredibly, bring him east, to this moment in history. What's more, the view from the Capitol's western steps allowed a backward glance at the nation's past even as it inspired thoughts of new beginnings: when Reagan rose to deliver his first speech as president, he would look out on a landscape cluttered with images from the nation's history—the memorials to George Washington and Abraham Lincoln, a hillside in the distance where an eternal flame marked the grave of John F.

Kennedy, the reflecting pool around which thousands had gathered to hear Martin Luther King speak of his dream. The White House was just to the north, to his right; the Jefferson Memorial to the south, on his left.

Ronald Reagan loved to allude to uplifting episodes in American history. Now, about to make history himself, he was surrounded by symbols of a heritage he embraced and hoped to draw upon in the coming years.

While the change of setting was intended to symbolize a fresh start, indeed, a break with the recent past, there was no escaping the shadow of unfinished business. As Reagan prepared to assume the nation's highest office, Americans were being held as hostages in Iran. Their plight and America's inability to force a resolution to the crisis helped sweep Reagan to victory over Jimmy Carter in 1980. With Carter's presidency about to come to an inglorious end, negotiations were underway to free the captive Americans.

No outgoing president in American history spent his last night in the White House working as hard as Jimmy Carter did. He spent the night, and the night before that, monitoring his dying administration's last-ditch efforts to free the fifty-two hostages. Washington was in the process of releasing $12 billion in Iranian assets frozen since the hostage crisis began in late 1979. In return, the Iranian government signaled that it would arrange for the hostages' safe passage home.

But when? Would the talks break down at the last minute? If not, would the hostages clear Iranian air space while Jimmy Carter still was president? Would the new president be able to announce an end to the crisis in his inaugural address?

Reagan took a phone call from Carter at eight-thirty on the morning of January 20, just a few hours before the ceremonies were to begin. The outgoing president was exhausted after a long, frustrating night—his last one in the White House. According to journalist Richard Reeves, Carter told Reagan that while everything was in place to bring the hostages home, they probably would not leave Iran until after the inaugural ceremonies were over. The airplanes were ready, but there was no sign of movement. Reagan would not have good news to announce in his inaugural address.[1]

Hours later, the two presidents, outgoing and incoming, shared the traditional drive together from the White House to the Capitol. They had little to say to each other. Several days earlier, Carter and his wife, Rosalynn, gave Reagan and his wife, Nancy, a tour of the White House living quarters, but after a few preliminaries, the Carters handed the task over to staff members and disappeared. The Reagans were insulted, adding to the strain between the defeated president and his successor. During the ride to the Capitol on Inauguration Day, Reagan tried to break the tension by regaling Carter with stories about his Hollywood days. Carter, not as conversant with popular culture circa 1945, as Reagan was, hardly responded. Later, Carter complained that Reagan spent the ride talking about somebody named Jack Warner, who, of course, was the legendary head of Warner Brothers studio. "Who's Jack Warner?" Carter asked.[2]

Carter's mood on inaugural morning may have had less to do with lingering bitterness towards Reagan than with simple exhaustion, as Reagan himself would acknowledge years later. It was not the best of times for the man from Georgia. Not only had he been rejected at the polls in a landslide in November, but his last days as president were among the most dramatic of his administration. The crisis that helped end his presidency still was not over, and, in fact, some of his top aides remained in the White House to monitor the situation at the airport in Teheran even as Carter accompanied Reagan to the Capitol for the inaugural ceremony.

The situation in Iran remained so fluid that as Reagan rose to take the oath of office from Chief Justice Warren Burger, he glanced at Carter to see if anything had changed, if the hostages had been released yet and were on their way home. According to Reeves's account of the ceremony in his book, *President Reagan*, Carter shook his head and whispered "Not yet"—his last words as president.[3]

The midday sun warmed Reagan's face as he placed his left hand on his mother's Bible, open to one of Nelle Wilson Reagan's favorite verses, 2 Chronicles 7:14: "If my people, which are called by my name, shall humble themselves, and pray, and seek my face, and turn from their wicked ways, then will I hear from heaven, and will forgive their sin, and will heal their land." The new president and the old differed in style, personality, and ideology, but both shared a deep faith in God. Reagan attributed his faith to his mother, "a small woman with auburn hair and a sense of optimism that ran as deep as the cosmos," he wrote.[4] She believed the hand of God was behind life's disappointments and its triumphs. Her son took the lesson to heart.

He had hoped to begin his speech with news of the hostages' return to freedom. Instead, after paying homage to the nation's "orderly transfer of power," he praised Carter for his cooperation in that transfer—a rare gesture in American inaugural rhetoric. Carter himself had thanked his vanquished opponent, Gerald Ford, in 1977. Before that, however, few new presidents had acknowledged the services of their predecessors.

"Mr. President," Reagan said, addressing himself directly to Carter, "I want our fellow citizens to know how much you did to carry on" the tradition of orderly transitions. "By your gracious cooperation in the transition process, you have shown a watching world that we are a united people pledged to maintaining a political system which guarantees individual liberty to a greater degree than any other, and I thank you and your people for all your help in maintaining the continuity which is the bulwark of our Republic." Given the tension between the two men, Reagan's gesture was gracious, indeed.

Unspoken but implicit in Reagan's acknowledgment was Carter's unsparing efforts on behalf of the hostages in Iran. Reagan believed he should say nothing about the unfolding developments, fearing that the wrong word or even a public acknowledgement of the pending release might prompt a setback. In paying tribute to Carter's efforts during the transition, Reagan was really acknowledging the former president's role in leading the hostage negotiations.

Reagan then got to the business at hand: the economic malaise that had persuaded millions of voters to give his conservative, ideologically driven solutions a try. "These United States are confronted with an economic affliction of great proportions," he said. Few presidents have delivered such a blunt and unsparing assessment of the nation in his very first speech, but it was hardly a controversial assertion. The short-lived administrations of both of Reagan's immediate predecessors, Carter and Ford, tried and failed to tame soaring prices and rising unemployment.

"The economic ills we suffer have come upon us over several decades," he said. "They will not go away in days, weeks, or months, but they will go away. They will go away because we, as Americans, have the capacity now, as we have had in the past, to do whatever needs to be done to preserve this last and greatest bastion of freedom.

"In this present crisis, government is not the solution to our problem. Government is the problem."

It was an applause line, and Reagan paused to prompt the crowd's reaction. But among the thousands gathered to hear the new president were men and women of both parties whose world view was vastly different from Reagan's, and whose applause must have been perfunctory at best. Longtime members of Congress, former cabinet officers, federal administrators, lobbyists, and dependable campaign contributors all had a vested interest in the status quo that Reagan challenged. They believed in the power of the federal government to provide solutions that seemed beyond the capabilities of private enterprise. The New Deal saved capitalism from itself; World War II and the Cold War enhanced government's interventions in the economy, and the social transformations of the 1960s and '70s led to federal programs to aid the poor, educate the nation's children, support the arts, protect the environment, and enhance civil rights.

The Washington political establishment, Republicans and Democrats alike, had heard complaints about the growth and power of the federal government since Franklin Roosevelt's presidency. Reagan's insistence that government did not have the answers to the crises of the 1980s was not new. He had said as much during the campaign, and Barry Goldwater had said as much in 1964.

This time, however, the argument sounded a good deal more powerful, because the man who made it was not just a conservative critic, not just an articulate ideologue. The man who saw no place for government in solving the nation's economic crisis was, in fact, the head of the government. And yet, he saw himself as a nonpolitician, or even an antipolitician, a man who had none of the great affection for government and its practitioners that so many members of Congress, lobbyists, and journalists had. They knew people like Reagan, but they tended to be people who wrote angry letters to the editor, and who embarked on quixotic campaigns for local offices. They did not take the oath of office as president of the United States. Until now.

"It is my intention to curb the size and influence of the federal establishment and to demand recognition of the distinction between the powers granted to the federal government and those reserved to the States or to the people," he said. "All of us need to be reminded that the Federal Government did not create the States; the States created the Federal Government."

Although Reagan understood the power of language better than any president since John Kennedy, and while some of his most dramatic speeches would be remembered for their grace and beauty, in his first speech as president, Reagan was determined not to inspire but to establish the parameters of a new order. Flights of rhetoric were suited for ceremony; this was the first act of a political revolution, and Reagan framed it as such with spare, clear, and direct language.

"Now, so there will be no misunderstanding, it is not my intention to do away with government," he said, no doubt to the relief of the political establishment gathered around him. "It is, rather, to make it work—work with us, not over us; to stand by our side, not ride our back. Government can and must provide opportunity, not smother it; foster productivity, not stifle it."

The heroes of Ronald Reagan's revolution would not be legislators or other political officials. They would be the very Americans whose confidence Jimmy Carter found wanting during a famous speech in 1979, when he announced that the nation was suffering from a "crisis of confidence." Reagan saw not a demoralized nation, but a nation of heroes. "Those who say that we are in a time when there are no heroes, they just don't know where to look," he said, flexing his rhetorical muscles on behalf not of politicians but of ordinary Americans. "You meet heroes across a counter— and they are on both sides of that counter. There are entrepreneurs with faith in themselves and faith in an idea who create new jobs, new wealth, and opportunity. They are individuals and families whose taxes support the governor and whose voluntary gifts support church, charity, culture, art, and education. Their patriotism is quiet but deep. Their values sustain our national life."

Those values, he said, would see the nation through its crisis, because they were exceptional values born of an exceptional nation. These were not sentiments often heard in the early 1980s, but Reagan firmly believed them. Americans, he said, "can and will resolve the problems which now confront us. And, after all, why shouldn't they believe that? We are Americans."

For Ronald Reagan, there was no better explanation.

Ronald Reagan and Jimmy Carter seated in the presidential limousine on their way to Reagan's inauguration

Ronald Reagan addresses Congress for the first time after the assassination attempt

CHAPTER 7

The President Has Become a Hero

The First Speech after the Assassination Attempt

April 28, 1981

TRACK 7

OR THE NEW REAGAN ADMINISTRATION, THE ECONOMY TRUMPED ALL OTHER concerns and issues, including the Cold War. The president's inaugural address made it clear that a simple or quick fix wouldn't do—even if one could be found. Ronald Reagan wanted to bring about a profound change in the relationship between the government and the private sector, and he was prepared to expend political capital to bring about that change.

On March 30, 1981, the president brought his agenda to an audience that was not accustomed to hearing from probusiness, tax-cutting Republicans. The Building and Construction Trades Department of the AFL-CIO, the nation's largest labor union, was heavily Democratic and could be expected to be skeptical at best of Reagan's demands for less government intervention in the economy. Nevertheless, Reagan, never lacking for confidence in his ability to persuade and charm, chose to address the union's leaders and rank and file during a national conference in the Washington Hilton Hotel.

The president's audience knew what to expect, for Reagan already had followed up his inaugural with a nationally televised speech on the economy on February 5. That speech began with a stark assessment of the nation's woes: "I regret to say that we're in the worst economic mess since the Great

Depression." Reagan went on to cite an array of statistics to back up his dire assertion. The nation, he said, "just had two years of back-to-back double-digit inflation—13.3 percent in 1979, 12.4 percent last year. The last time this happened was in World War I." Seven million people were "caught up in the personal indignity and human tragedy of unemployment," he continued. Young Americans could no longer afford to buy their first home, thanks to mortgage interest rates of 15.4 percent.[1]

The main culprits, Reagan said, were excessive government regulations, which increased the cost of doing business, and mounting federal deficits, which drove up interest rates.

Reagan's February 5 speech addressed a national crisis, but unlike Jimmy Carter, Reagan did not blame his fellow Americans for the nation's bleak condition. Carter famously, or infamously, diagnosed a "crisis of confidence" in America in 1979. Reagan, confronting many of the same economic problems, portrayed American workers as the victims rather than the agents of the nation's crisis. "I'll match the American working man or woman against anyone in the world," he said. "But we have to give them the tools and equipment that workers in other industrial nations have." That goal could be achieved, he said, by getting government out of the way of business.

Reagan's nationwide address carried a sense of urgency—"We're out of time," he said, referring to the need to find long-term solutions to the nation's economic woes. He wanted to reiterate that message to the building and trades union conference. Wearing a brand-new blue suit, Reagan began by reminding the union that he was a lifetime member of the AFL-CIO by virtue of leadership of the Screen Actors Guild. He had negotiated contracts with management. He knew "the meaning of work and of family and of country." That, he hoped, gave him the standing to tell his audience that the system simply wasn't working, and that most of America—including unionized workers—"wants a change."

Reagan spoke for about twenty minutes, generating polite applause. He left the hotel's ballroom at about 2:25 p.m. and was escorted to a side exit on T Street NW, where his limousine was parked. Flanked by Secret Service agents and followed by several aides, the president walked briskly past the usual retinue of television cameras and reporters. Somebody yelled out a question. Then, to the president's left, came a popping sound. A man named

John Hinckley Jr. fired four shots from a .22 caliber handgun at the president's party. Reagan turned towards the sound. "What the hell's that?" he said just as Secret Service agent Jerry Parr flung himself forward, grabbed the president around the waist, and pushed him into the limousine.[2] The car sped away as Hinckley was wrestled to the ground. James Brady, Reagan's press secretary, lay face down on the sidewalk, blood streaming from a head wound. Two other men, Secret Service agent Tim McCarthy and Washington police officer Tom Delehanty, were also wounded, although not as severely as Brady.

Reagan didn't realize it, but one of Hinckley's bullets hit him under his left arm and was lodged an inch from his heart. He was bleeding from his mouth and had trouble breathing, but he assumed Parr had broken one of his ribs when he flung him into the limo. He was rushed to George Washington Hospital; incredibly, given his condition, he insisted on walking into the emergency room. But after about twenty feet, his will gave way to the gravity of his wound. He was helped onto a gurney, his new suit was cut off his body, and doctors began inserting tubes into his body. He passed out briefly, but revived when he felt a soft hand in his—the hand of a nurse named Marisa Mize. "Who's holding my hand?" he asked. "Who's holding my hand? Does Nancy know about us?"[3] Not long afterwards, Nancy Reagan was at her husband's side. "Honey," Reagan said, "I forgot to duck."[4]

Ronald Reagan nearly died that afternoon. His chest cavity was filled with blood, making it impossible for him to breathe on his own. He managed another joke before undergoing surgery, telling a doctor, Joseph Giordano, that he hoped he was a Republican. "Today, Mr. President, we're all Republicans," the doctor replied.[5]

Reagan was in far worse condition than the public was being told, and that remained true during his recovery. Amid the chaos that afternoon, Reagan's secretary of state, Alexander Haig, told an anxious nation that he was "in control" because Vice President George Bush was not in Washington—he was flying back from Texas. The Constitution gave him authority to serve in place of the president and vice president, Haig said, but the document actually listed the Speaker of the House and temporary President of the Senate, in that order, ahead of the secretary of state.

The president's recovery was not nearly as smooth as press reports indicated, but within ten days his temperature was normal and he was working a bit. Stories about his courage and his wit transformed his presidency even as he lay in a hospital bed. Before the shooting, he had a mandate from the people. Now, it seemed as though the mandate came from a higher source. He returned to the White House on April 11, and not long afterwards, he wrote in his diary: "Whatever happens now I owe my life to God and will try to serve him in every way I can."[6] Reagan's approval rating skyrocketed to nearly 80 percent.

Although he remained weak, Reagan began working the phones to cajole members of the House to support legislation to slash federal spending—which meant, for many members, possible cuts to favorite projects that helped them look good to the voters back home. Such cuts were anathema to politicians with eyes fixed on the next election, never far away for House members. But now they were being asked to put aside self-interest and support not a president, but an authentic folk hero.

The stage was set for Ronald Reagan's first official public appearance since being shot. He no longer looked like a very sick, very weak elderly gentleman: he regained the dozen pounds he lost while in the hospital, his ruddy complexion was back, and so was his energy.

A joint session of Congress assembled in the House chamber on the night of April 28 to witness the return of Ronald Reagan from near-death. When he entered the chamber, men and women rose from their seats and cheered as millions of Americans watched on television. The cheers came from Democrats and Republicans alike, from liberals and conservatives. Later, Reagan would say that the reception "was almost worth getting shot."[7] The rituals of politics demand that politicians show signs of respect for the presidency even when they disagree with the occupant of the office. On this occasion, though, the cheers were not for the office, but for the man.

When his audience finally was seated, and as Vice President Bush and House Speaker Tip O'Neill watched from their places behind him, Reagan thanked the nation for "your prayers, not only for me but for those others who fell beside me."

He had, as he would always seem to have, a homey anecdote designed to charm and disarm his listeners. He mentioned a letter he received from a second-grader named Peter Sweeney, who said he hoped the president got well soon "or you might have to make a speech in your pajamas." The crowd laughed, and Reagan quickly segued from his health to the economy.

"Thanks to some very fine people," he said, "my health is much improved. I'd like to be able to say that with regard to the health of the economy."

Six months had passed since his election, he noted. But nothing had changed. Inflation remained in double digits, and so did mortgage interest rates. Eight million people were out of work. Wages were lower on that night than they had been on election night because of the draining effect of inflation. The time had come to do something—not just anything, but something different.

"The American people now want us to act and not in half-measures," he said. "They demand and they've earned a full and comprehensive effort to clean up our economic mess. Because of the extent of the economy's sickness, we know that the cure will not come quickly and that even with our package, progress will come in inches and feet, not in miles."

As his audience knew, Reagan came to Capitol Hill on this event not simply to display his recovery or to tell warm and fuzzy stories about well-wishers. He had a specific mission: to persuade members of the House to vote for a budget bill sponsored by Representatives Phil Gramm of Texas, a Democrat, and Del Latta of Ohio, a Republican, rather than one drawn up by the Democratic-controlled House Budget Committee. Reagan said the Budget Committee measure would "leave spending too high and tax rates too high. At the same time, I think it cuts the defense budget too much, and by attempting to reduce the deficit through higher taxes, it will not create the kind of strong economic growth and the new jobs we must have."

"The old and comfortable way is to shave a little here and add a little there," Reagan said. "Well, that's not acceptable anymore. I think this great and historic Congress knows that way is no longer acceptable."

Determined to turn the country in a new direction, convinced that bold change and courage were needed, Reagan turned to the recent success of the first space shuttle mission, which took off and landed while the president was recuperating. It was the nation's first manned space voyage in six years.

"The space shuttle did more than prove our technological abilities," he said, subtly linking his economic plan to America's patriotism and latent sense of mission. "It raised our expectations once more. It started us dreaming again. The poet Carl Sandburg wrote, 'The republic is a dream. Nothing happens unless first a dream.' And that's what makes us, as

Americans, different. We've always reached for a new spirit and aimed at a higher goal. We've been courageous and determined, unafraid and bold." Such words, from a man who had joked with doctors on a hospital gurney, a bullet near his heart, profoundly moved his silent listeners. "Who among us wants to be the first to say we no longer have those qualities, that we must limp along, doing the same things that have brought us our present misery?

"I believe that the people you and I represent are ready to chart a new course … All we need to have is faith … All we need to do is act, and the time for action is now."

His audience rose and cheered again. The fledgling Reagan Revolution became not just another political program, but a mythic adventure led by a brave and determined captain.

The Speaker of the House and ranking Democrat in Washington, Tip O'Neill, acknowledged that after the president left Capitol Hill that night, resistance was futile. "The president has become a hero," O'Neill said. "We can't argue with a man as popular as he is."[8]

Nevertheless, O'Neill tried his best to argue with the popular president. Weeks of passionate politicking in the press and behind closed doors ended with a presidential victory in July, when Congress passed a budget calling for a 25 percent cut in federal income taxes over three years along with an increase in military spending. "Now we must make it work," Reagan wrote in his diary, "and we will."[9]

Ronald Reagan returns home to the White House after his recovery

Ronald Reagan speaks to the press about the striking air traffic controllers

CHAPTER 8

Breaking a Union

Press Conference on the
Air Controllers' Strike
August 3, 1981

TRACK 8

RONALD REAGAN DELIGHTED IN POINTING OUT THAT HE WAS THE ONLY president of the United States who had served as a union leader and, therefore, the only president who ever led a strike. Not long after he resigned as president of the Screen Actors Guild in 1960, he was asked if he thought his union activities hurt his acting career. He said he didn't think so, but he conceded that studio management might have come to think of him not as an actor but as "the guy who sat across the conference table, beefing."[1]

Despite Reagan's experience as a labor leader and his lifetime membership in the AFL-CIO, most of the nation's unions spurned him in 1980. That wasn't altogether surprising, despite Reagan's record as a labor leader. Unions were an important part of the Democratic Party's base since the New Deal, and while local Republicans occasionally won the support of organized labor, the party's presidential candidates generally could expect little support from union leaders.

But there was one exception: the Professional Air Traffic Controllers Organization (PATCO) broke ranks with its union brothers and sisters in 1980 by endorsing Reagan. The union's president, Robert Poli, met with Reagan during the campaign and received a letter from the candidate pledging to work together in the coming years in an effort to improve air safety.

The controllers were employees of the Federal Aviation Administration, so their support for Reagan was significant. They were not only defying other unions with their endorsement, they were defying their ultimate boss, President Carter. It was a gamble, but when Reagan won, so, seemingly, did PATCO and its nearly eighteen thousand members. They had a friend in the White House—a friend who was proud to remind people of his own record as a union leader.

PATCO and the FAA opened talks for a new contract in February. The union wanted a pay increase of ten thousand dollars a year for each of its members along with a reduction in the workweek from five days and forty hours to four days and thirty-two hours. Citing the job's incredible stress, the union also asked for full retirement benefits after twenty years of service. The total package was estimated at about $700 million over three years.

Talks between the union and the FAA continued through the spring and summer. While the president was kept informed of the negotiations from time to time, he was a busy man during those formative months of his administration. In the midst of the titanic battle over his budget, he made good on a campaign promise by nominating Sandra Day O'Connor, a judge from Arizona, to become the first woman Supreme Court justice. Events abroad also commanded his attention, as the Soviet Union massed troops on the Polish border while a fledgling union movement in Poland called Solidarity challenged the Communist government in Warsaw.

In late July, Poli, the PATCO president, announced that an overwhelming majority of his members rejected the FAA's offer of a $40 million package of raises and other concessions. Reagan's secretary of transportation, Drew Lewis, announced that the government would not budge on its offer. Confident that concern about air safety would persuade their friends in the White House to make a better offer, PATCO's leaders authorized a strike for seven o'clock in the morning, eastern time, on August 3—the height of the summer travel season. Federal law banned strikes by its employees, but postal workers and other workers had gone on strike or carried out job actions without suffering any legal penalties. Likewise, workers in local and municipal governments—most prominently in New York City—had gone on strike in recent years despite similar bans. They returned to their jobs after winning new contracts.

So when the White House did not put forward a better offer, more than twelve thousand air traffic controllers walked off the job at the appointed hour. Several thousand supervisors, military employees, and dissident union members were left to man the vacated towers. The FAA ordered airlines to cut their flights by half.

Just before ten o'clock that morning, President Reagan addressed members of the press in the Rose Garden. It was, he would later say, "the first real national emergency I faced as president."[2] The strike threatened to paralyze not just the summer tourist industry, but business travel and cargo traffic. Tens of millions of dollars in fresh food and other goods would be lost even in a short strike. And the airline industry employed more than three hundred thousand people. If airplanes couldn't fly, the toll on the nation's economy would be enormous.

Reagan, of course, respected labor's right to strike, having led SAG's strike in 1960. But he drew a distinction between the private sector and the public sector. It was one thing to shut down the movie industry or a manufacturing plant, he believed. It was another to endanger the public. One of his heroes and role models was Calvin Coolidge, who, as governor of Massachusetts, refused to approve the rehiring of Boston police officers who had walked off their jobs in 1919. Coolidge famously said that nobody had a right to strike against the public's safety. Reagan agreed, and said so.

As he faced the White House press corps, Reagan read from a handwritten statement he had drafted the night before. He focused first not on the illegality of the strike, but on the economic demands of the union. The controllers, he said, had rejected a $40 million increase in wages and benefits, "twice what other government employees can expect." Their demands for some $700 million in raises and benefits "would impose a tax burden on their fellow citizens which is unacceptable." At a time of economic discontent, in an antitax atmosphere that the president himself had stirred up, Reagan focused on the size of the union's demand, and on the fact that the money it demanded would have to come from the taxpayers. It was a deliberate and effective way to isolate the controllers from other workers, including other union members.

Only after citing the union's demands did Reagan focus on the strike's impact on public safety and its defiance of federal law. He read from "the solemn oath taken by each of these employees, a sworn affidavit, when they accepted their jobs." The oath required employees to promise that they "will not participate" in strikes against the government.

For Reagan, the issue was simple: the controllers violated the law when they went on strike. They had put the public's safety at risk in pursuit of what he considered to be unreasonable remands.

"It is for this reason," he read, "that I must tell those who fail to report for duty this morning they are in violation of the law, and if they do not report for work within 48 hours, they have forfeited their jobs and will be terminated."

Ronald Reagan was not bluffing.

After he finished his statement, Attorney General William French Smith and Transportation Secretary Lewis stepped forward to assist the president with reporters' questions about punishments, whether the government planned to hire replacement workers, and whether the administration planned to sweeten its offer to the union before the president's deadline expired. The answers were not good for the union: the Justice Department planned to begin criminal proceedings against PATCO, it would hire replacement workers, and there would be no better offer forthcoming.

At eleven o'clock on Wednesday, August 5, twelve thousand air traffic controllers were fired by order of the president. The mass disruption that the union was counting on never happened. There were no accidents, and within a week of the firings, about 80 percent of the nation's flights were proceeding as scheduled. At a press conference in California on August 13, a reporter asked Reagan about the strike. The president replied that there was no strike. The controllers, he said, had quit their jobs by refusing to show up for work.

Reagan's suppression of PATCO inspired no sympathy strikes from the controllers' brothers and sisters in organized labor. The public seemed to side with the president despite the inconvenience that cancelled or delayed flights and the union's assertions that Reagan was to blame for unfriendly skies.

While there is no indication that Ronald Reagan picked a fight with PATCO to serve notice on the nation's workers that they should submit to management's dictation, or else, many commentators have insisted the PATCO firings set a tone for labor-management relations in the years since. The number of strikes has decreased markedly, from about three hundred a year during the immediate post-war era to a double-digit handful per year since the PATCO walkout. When the United Auto Workers ordered what became a one-day strike against General Motors in 2007, it was the first such mass shutdown against the nation's largest carmaker since 1970.

In 1981, about a quarter of the nation's work force was unionized. By 2007, about 13 percent was. Unionized blue-collar jobs in industries like steel disappeared as companies moved plants to countries where labor was cheaper, while other industries, like automaking, saw its market share fall in the face of foreign competition.

It is hard to imagine that Ronald Reagan's busting of PATCO was to blame for the decline of union membership and worker militancy in the United States. But it also seems clear that his actions, like his budget, signaled a change in American political arrangements. Workers in the United States would continue to suffer job losses and other setbacks through the Reagan years. But rarely did the president get the blame.

A protestor wears a Ronald Reagan mask at a peace rally in Bonn, Germany

CHAPTER 9

The Zero Option

Remarks to the National Press Club
on Arms Reduction
November 18, 1981

TRACK 9

DOMESTIC POLICY WAS THE REAGAN ADMINISTRATION'S FIRST, SECOND, AND third priorities during its first year in office. The president's inaugural address and his first several major speeches made it clear that Reagan and his aides intended to use the energy and goodwill of their first few months in office to not simply slap a Band-Aid on the economy, but to implement fundamental changes in tax policy, spending priorities, and government regulation.

His aides were convinced that Reagan had little interest in foreign affairs, despite his reputation as an enthusiastic Cold Warrior. According to Reagan biographer Richard Reeves, Richard Cheney, a young congressman from Wyoming, was surprised by the president's apparent disinterest in events overseas. Cheney, according to Reeves, told a friend that the president didn't "seem to have the hunger" to assert himself on the global stage. "He does what he has to do and that's all."[1]

Reagan's travel log supported Cheney's analysis—there were no high-profile trips overseas during the president's first year in office. Reagan's focus on matters close to home became even more intense in the summer of 1981, when the nation officially slipped into an economic recession, one that would prove to be the worst such decline since the

Great Depression and would lead to a sharp decline in the president's approval ratings.

But it was wrong to conclude, as Cheney apparently did, that Reagan was simply going through the motions in foreign affairs. In the spring of 1981, as he sat in the White House solarium in his robe and pajamas recovering from his gunshot wounds, Reagan began to reflect on the state of Soviet-American relations. Nuclear arms negotiations were stalled, but the Soviets had sent a private message that they might be interested in returning to the negotiating table. The White House did not respond in kind at first, but as Reagan recuperated, he later wrote, he decided to "do whatever I could in the years God had given me to reduce the threat of nuclear war..."[2] He grabbed a pad of paper and began writing a private letter to Soviet leader Leonid Brezhnev.

Reagan wasn't sure he would actually send it, but he wanted at the very least to put his thoughts in writing. He wanted to resume talks about nuclear arms, and he wanted to end the U.S. boycott of grain shipments to the Soviets, implemented during the Carter administration to protest the Russian invasion of Afghanistan. When Reagan told Secretary of State Al Haig about the letter, Haig was aghast. Any such communication, he said, ought to be drafted by the State Department. In his autobiography, Reagan wrote that it was at this moment when he realized that Haig didn't "want me as the president to be involved in setting foreign policy—he regarded it as his turf; he wanted to formulate it and carry it out himself."[3] While Haig supported the idea of renewed arms control talks, he was opposed to ending the grain embargo.

A draft of the letter was sent to Haig's department, was put through the mill of diplomat-speak, and returned to Reagan for his approval. He did not approve—he felt the letter had been drained of its personal, human qualities. But he seemed resigned to the vetting process. "This isn't what I had written," he said to aide Michael Deaver, "but they are the experts." Deaver, who understood Reagan far better than Haig, was not about to allow his boss to give up so easily.

"You know, Mr. President," he said, "those assholes have been running the Soviet business for the last forty years, and they haven't done a very good job of it. None of them ever got elected to anything; you got elected. Why don't you just tell them to stick it and send the letter?"[4]

Reagan did just that, sort of: two letters were dispatched to Brezhnev. A formal letter criticized the Soviet's "unremitting and comprehensive [military] buildup" and accused it of seeking "military superiority." It also indicated that the United States did not believe the time was right for a summit meeting between the nations. Attached to the State Department-approved communication was the personal note Reagan wrote. Filled with sentiment and willing to ask sensitive questions of both superpowers, Reagan's letter informed Brezhnev that the United States would resume grain supplies with the hope that a "constructive dialogue" might follow.

Reagan reminded the Soviet leader that they had met in San Clemente years earlier, when Brezhnev visited then-President Nixon for a summit that "captured the imagination of all the world. Never had peace and good will among men seemed closer at hand."[5] Coming from Ronald Reagan, such a nostalgic view of the beginnings of détente surely must have taken the Soviets by surprise.

Reagan went on:

Is it possible that we have permitted ideology, political and economic philosophies, and governmental policies to keep us from considering the very real, everyday problems of peoples? ... When World War II ended, the United States had the only undamaged industrial power in the world ... If we had sought world domination, then who could have opposed us? But the United States followed a different course—one unique in all of the history of mankind. We used our power and wealth to rebuild the war-ravaged economies of the world, including those who had been our enemies. May I say there is absolutely no substance to charges that the United States is guilty of imperialism ...

The United States and Soviets, Reagan suggested, ought to be "eliminating the obstacles which prevent our people from achieving their most cherished" goals.

The Soviets replied to this olive branch with a chilly letter saying only that they, too, believed the time was not right for a summit meeting. "So much for my first attempt at personal diplomacy," Reagan later wrote.[6] But before long, both nations agreed to resume arms talks in late November.

Despite the setback, Reagan continued to think about challenging the Cold War status quo even as he pressed forward with his domestic agenda. The summer of 1981 found Washington in the midst of a memorable political conflict between Reagan and Speaker O'Neill over the president's first budget. All the while, it was impossible to shunt aside events overseas. In August, President Anwar Sadat of Egypt paid a state visit to the White House just as the Reagan administration was discussing how to react to Libyan harassment of U.S. planes and ships over and in the Mediterranean Sea. Sadat, according to Reagan, was delighted to learn that the United States was preparing naval and air maneuvers off the Libyan coast as a show of strength. On August 20, after Sadat left, two Libyan warplanes fired at U.S. F-14s. The Libyans missed their target; the F-14s did not.

Two months later, Islamic fundamentalists assassinated Sadat for his role in making peace with Israel. Reagan believed the Libyan leader, Muammar al-Qaddafi, was responsible for Sadat's death or at least knew about it in advance.

Reagan was scheduled to deliver remarks at a meeting of the National Press Club, a group of Washington-based reporters, in late November. It was time, he decided, to make a formal statement of some of the issues he had been thinking about since the assassination attempt. Reagan's cabinet was divided about the president's willingness to offer incentives to the Soviets in an effort to reduce the possibility of nuclear war. Reagan favored what became known as the "zero option"—the total elimination of intermediate-range nuclear missiles in Europe. To achieve that goal, he was willing to cancel his controversial plan to install new U.S. Pershing and cruise missiles in Europe if the Soviets promised to dismantle the SS-20, SS-4, and SS-5 intermediate-range missiles in Eastern Europe. Haig opposed the idea, while Secretary of Defense Caspar Weinberger supported it.

After hearing the pros and cons, Reagan took a flight aboard the special airborne presidential command center designed for use in the event of a nuclear attack. Called the "doomsday plane," it was a specially designed 747 with no windows and stuffed with all kinds of blinking communications devices. It reminded the president of a submarine.

During the flight, Reagan decided to go forward with his zero option proposal. He would reveal it during his appearance at the Press Club.

The major television networks were on hand to broadcast the speech live, although the timing—the president began speaking at ten o'clock in the morning—did not suggest that there would be much news value in the speech. But Reagan would later say that he never gave such an important speech on foreign policy.

As he approached a podium inside the National Press Club building, Reagan looked a little thicker around the torso. He was wearing a bulky bulletproof vest, a precaution taken after U.S. intelligence picked up a report that a Libyan agent was in the United States and had orders to kill the president. A battalion of Secret Service agents lined the room. The show of force was a relief to Reagan, just six months removed from John Hinckley's assassination attempt. If the Libyan agent really existed, he'd have a hard time executing his mission in the presence of so much security.

Reagan began the speech by quoting at length from his personal letter to Brezhnev, which he believed set the tone for what he was about to say. "Twice in my lifetime, I have seen the peoples of Europe plunged into the tragedy of war," he said. "All of us who lived through those troubled times share a common resolve that they must never come again."

For decades now, he noted, that Atlantic alliance had prevented the scourge of war from returning to Europe. Reagan affirmed the U.S. commitment to the North Atlantic Treaty Organization and praised its efforts in maintaining peace. However, NATO now faced a new threat in the form of Soviet intermediate-range nuclear missiles pointed at the nations of Western Europe. Offering a history lesson as a build up to his main proposal, Reagan noted that the NATO allies agreed to respond to the Soviet buildup with one of their own in 1979—before he took office. "Deployment of these [weapons] systems will demonstrate to the Soviet Union" that the alliance would not be broken, he said.

As the United States and the Soviets prepared to face each other at the bargaining table in two weeks, Reagan said, he wished to send Brezhnev another "simple, straightforward yet historic message. The United States proposes the mutual reduction of conventional intermediate-range nuclear and strategic forces." The proposal would require four steps, none more surprising than the first.

"I have informed President Brezhnev that ... [the] United States is prepared to cancel its deployment of Pershing II and ground-launch cruise missiles if the Soviets will dismantle their SS-20, SS-4, and SS-5 missiles.

This would be an historic step. With Soviet agreement, we could together substantially reduce the dread threat of nuclear war which hangs over the people of Europe. This, like the first footstep on the moon, would be a giant step for mankind."

It was a giant leap, for an administration perceived to be provocative and bellicose after the years of Cold War détente. It also was a shrewd political step to counter the march of the nuclear freeze movement, which opposed the U.S. deployment and was gathering mainstream support in both Europe and the United States.

Reagan also announced that he wished to change the focus of the upcoming round of arms control talks. Previous rounds were known as the Strategic Arms Limitation Talks, or SALT. Nuclear limitation, however, was no longer enough for Reagan. He wished for more drastic changes. "To symbolize this fundamental change in direction," he said, "we will call these negotiations START—Strategic Arms Reduction Talks."

"There is no reason why people in any part of the world should have to live in permanent fear of war or its specter," Reagan said. "I believe the time has come for all nations to act in a responsible spirit that doesn't threaten other states. I believe the time is right to move forward on arms control and the resolution of critical regional disputes at the conference table. Nothing will have a higher priority for me and for the American people over the coming months and years."

He finished with a quote from John F. Kennedy, another president whose early militant rhetoric grew softer in the face of Cold War calculations of body counts. Reagan recalled that "another American president described the goal that we still pursue today. He said: 'If we can persevere, if we can look beyond our shores and ambitions, then surely the age will dawn in which the strong are just and the weak secure and the peace preserved.'"

That president, he noted, didn't live to see that goal achieved. "I invite all nations," Reagan said, "to join with America today in the quest for such a world." The zero option did indeed become reality, but not before years of struggle and turmoil. Both the allies and the Soviets continued the missile buildup in Europe throughout the 1980s. But it was Kennedy who said, after all, that ambitious goals are worth pursuing "not because they are easy, but because they are hard."

Ronald Reagan addresses reporters at the National Press Club

Ronald Reagan speaks on the lawn of the White House next to Margaret Thatcher

CHAPTER 10

The Ash Heap of History

Address to the British Parliament
June 8, 1982

TRACK 10

B Y THE SPRING OF 1982, THE PRESS OF WORLD EVENTS DEMANDED THE president's utmost attention. Conflicts in South America and the Middle East, confrontations in Poland between workers and the Communist government, and mass protests against U.S. nuclear policy in Europe required the administration's response. In early June, Reagan flew to Europe for a crucial series of speeches and meetings with allies and trading partners. The trip, his first to the continent as president, would take him to Paris, Rome, London, Bonn, and Berlin even as events overseas appeared to be spinning out of his control.

A week before Reagan left for Europe, war broke out between Britain and Argentina over control of the Falkland Islands, a lonely colonial outpost off the South American coast. Two architects of Reagan's foreign policy, Secretary of State Alexander Haig and United Nations Ambassador Jeanne Kirkpatrick, disagreed on a U.N. resolution calling for a cease-fire, setting in motion a series of disputes that would lead to Haig's resignation in late June. In the Middle East, Israel launched an invasion of Lebanon just after the president touched down in France. Poland had been living under martial law ever since the Communist government arrested leaders of the labor union, Solidarity, the previous December. And huge crowds of demonstrators on both sides of the Atlantic, the largest since the turbulent 1960s, were gathering to protest construction of a new generation of U.S. nuclear missiles in Western Europe to counter a Soviet buildup. The demonstrators demanded that both the Soviets and the United States freeze their nuclear arsenals at current levels, a demand that, if implemented, would have scuttled installation of new U.S. missiles.

In the midst of these crises, Reagan's foreign policy and national security teams were feuding with each other over policy and personality. Haig's stock within the administration had been plummeting ever since he declared himself in control when the president was shot in March 1981. Haig wanted Kirkpatrick to abstain from a vote on a U.S. Security Council resolution which called for a British and Argentine cease-fire, but his directive arrived minutes after Kirkpatrick vetoed the resolution. Kirkpatrick publicly accused the State Department of incompetence. Meanwhile, the president's new national security advisor, William Clark, had absolutely no experience on foreign affairs; his appointment was widely derided internationally and at home.

But at this critical moment, as the president sought to introduce himself to skeptical Europeans and to reframe debate over American nuclear policy, he could count on the support and encouragement of one crucial European ally—British Prime Minister Margaret Thatcher. Time and circumstance had come together to create a moment when the leaders of the United Kingdom and the United States were virtually of one mind on both Cold War and economic issues. Thatcher, a grocer's daughter who had risen in 1979 to become Britain's first woman prime minister, promised voters to put an end Britain's decline as a global power. Like Reagan, she sought to roll back a half-century or more of government intervention in the economy, and like Reagan, she believed in a renewed confrontation with Soviet Communism.

But there was another historic figure in Europe who was destined to become a strategic partner of Reagan, and the president paid a call on him on June 7, 1982. Pope John Paul II commanded no troops, as Josef Stalin observed about the papacy a half-century earlier, and he presided over no great nation-state. But as the spiritual leader of nearly a billion Catholics, and as a native of Poland who bitterly resented Soviet control over his country, John Paul was a global figure of tremendous strategic importance for the United States.

Like Reagan, John Paul was once an actor. And, like Reagan, he still bore the scars of an assassination attempt. The pontiff was shot two months after the attempt on Reagan's life, while riding through St. Peter's Square. His recovery was as remarkable as Reagan's was, and as he greeted the president and his wife, the pontiff looked strong and athletic, a far cry from the tragic, stooped figure he became in later life. He clasped Nancy Reagan's right hand and grasped the president's right elbow as photographers recorded the moment. Not long afterwards, president and pontiff conferred privately about the U.S. nuclear strategy in Europe. After they reemerged, Reagan spoke of "the martyred nation of Poland" and promised to press the Polish government to end martial law. The pope, as many leaders would come to realize during his long reign, was not given to platitudes even on such ceremonial occasions. While polite, he reminded the president that "the scale and the horror of modern warfare, whether nuclear or not, makes it totally unacceptable as a means of settling differences between nations." It seemed like a pointed remark aimed at a president perceived to be preparing for war with the Soviets. In fact, Reagan shared the Pope's horror.

Reagan flew from Rome to London that afternoon, and the following day, June 8, he addressed members of the British Parliament—or most of them, anyway. Nearly all of the more than two hundred representatives of the Labour Party boycotted Reagan's appearance to protest America's nuclear buildup in Europe. If nothing else, the absence of the opposition meant that Reagan received a friendly hearing from an audience made up almost entirely of Mrs. Thatcher's Conservative Party.

The setting, the Royal Gallery in Westminster Palace, was both spare and visually rich. Reagan stood at a very ordinary lectern, several feet in front of an unattractive yellow curtain. But deployed on either side of the president was a contingent of Beefeaters dressed in their medieval uniforms—frilly white collars, red and gold coats, and black hats. Several troops held long pikes. It was a far cry from the security detail that usually protected the president, with their dark suits, sunglasses, and considerably more lethal armament. Seated on either side of the president were bewigged Parliamentary officers in their ceremonial black robes.

While both Britain and the United States were in the midst of conservative revolutions in domestic policy, Reagan chose not to speak about those similarities. Instead, he sought to revive the notion of Anglo-American solidarity in the face of a common enemy, Soviet Communism, whose downfall he believed was imminent. "In an ironic sense, Karl Marx was right," Reagan said. "We are witnessing today a great revolutionary crisis, a crisis where the demands of the economic order are conflicting directly with those of the political order. But the crisis is happening not in the free, non-Marxist West, but in the home of Marxist-Leninism, the Soviet Union." The Soviets, he said, were "in deep economic difficulty" and in "decay."

Reagan did not cite much in the way of hard evidence to support his claim, although he noted that a fifth of the Soviet nation was employed in agriculture, but still the nation had to import food. His assertion was based, then, not so much on economic data, but on common sense: ordinary people are bound to resist systems of oppression. He declared, "Since the exodus from Egypt, historians have written of those who sacrificed and struggled for freedom—the stand at Thermopylae, the revolt of Spartacus, the storming of the Bastille, the Warsaw Uprising in World War II," he said.

The struggle against Communism and totalitarianism, then, was part of this ongoing narrative of struggle against oppression. That narrative was being written not only in Europe, Reagan said, but in El Salvador, then embroiled in a brutal civil war between the government and leftist guerillas. "More recently," he said, "we've seen evidence of this same human impulse in one of the developing nations in Central America." The media, he said, had portrayed the rebels in El Salvador as liberators, with the government wielding the hammer of repression. But the opposite was true, Reagan argued. The government was holding off "Cuban-backed guerillas who want power for themselves, and their backers, not democracy for the people." Reagan took note of recent elections in El Salvador, saying that their success proved that democracy would win out over the violence of the leftist rebels. In fact, the carnage would continue in El Salvador for another decade, with government-backed death squads taking a fearsome toll.

Reagan said the same narrative of freedom was at work thousands of miles to the south, in the Falkland Islands. Whatever doubts his audience may have had about El Salvador—Reagan's support for the military regime became increasingly unpopular in Europe through the 1980s—the members of Parliament were delighted to hear praise for Britain's little war in the South Atlantic. Reagan acknowledged that "voices have been raised" in protest over a war "for lumps of rock and earth so far away." But Britain's soldiers were not fighting for real estate, he said. "They fight for a cause—for the belief that armed aggression must not be allowed to succeed …" Had Europe been as firm as Mrs. Thatcher was in the face of aggression, he said, "perhaps our generation wouldn't have suffered the bloodletting of World War II." The MPs interrupted with applause for the first and only time until he was done.

After years of détente with the Soviets, during which, in Reagan's view, the Communist threat became only more menacing, the president was preparing allies and the public not only for a vast buildup that would include new missiles in Europe, but a comprehensive program to promote democracy and destabilize Communist regimes. "The objective I propose is quite simple to state: to foster the infrastructure of democracy—the system of a free press, unions, political parties, universities—which allows a people to choose their own way to develop their own culture, to reconcile their own differences through peaceful means," he said. The Soviets were giving "covert political training and assistance to Marxist-Leninists in many countries." Now, he said, was the time to respond in kind. He invited the Soviet leader, the aging, ill Leonid Brezhnev, to address the American people on national television, if the Soviets would allow Reagan the same access to the Russian people.

"What I am describing now," he said, "is a plan … which will leave Marxism-Leninism on the ash heap of history …" But televised speeches and training sessions in the rituals of democracy would not be enough. New intermediate-range missiles were necessary, too, he said.

He ended, not unexpectedly, with a reverential reference to Winston Churchill. The great man once asked, at the very beginnings of the Cold War, "Why should we fear for our future? We have come safely through the worst."

Reagan, too, saw little reason for fear. "For the sake of peace and justice," he said, "let us move toward a world in which all people are at last free to determine their own destiny."

Back home, Reagan's speech to Parliament was dismissed as routine Cold War rhetoric. Time would show, however, that the speech was a work of prophesy.

Ronald Reagan and budget director David Stockman during a meeting in the Oval Office

CHAPTER 11

Staying the Course

Address to the
Nation on the Economy
October 13, 1982

TRACK 11

A S HIS SECOND YEAR IN OFFICE NEARED AN END, WITH AMERICANS ABOUT TO go to the polls for midterm congressional elections, Ronald Reagan was an embattled and unpopular figure. The economic turnaround he expected and predicted had not materialized. Although inflation was cut to just over 5 percent thanks to the Federal Reserve's tight money policies, prosperity had not followed the slashing of nondefense spending and the loosening of federal regulation. A long, deep recession began in 1981 and lingered like an unwelcome guest at a dinner party. Interest rates remained high, and with the national unemployment rate at just over 10 percent—the highest since 1940—Democratic critics began to describe the president's program as "Reaganomics." And Reagan's own budget director, David Stockman, told journalist William Greider of his doubts that the president's economic plan would work. Reagan later conceded that his program did not improve the nation's economy as quickly as he anticipated. In public, with the press describing the recession as the nation's worst economic downturn since the Depression, Reagan found himself on the defensive. He insisted that he had been stuck with an economic mess, but eventually "we'll work our way out of it."[1] Privately, he was engaged in a battle with staff and with himself over the issue of a tax increase to make up for falling revenues and increased defense spending. At first Reagan opposed the idea as precisely the sort of policy option he wanted to banish from Washington. "If I have to be criticized, I'd rather be criticized for a deficit rather than for backing away from our economic program," he wrote in his diary in early 1982.[2] In a moment of private reflection, he told aide Michael Deaver, "You know, Mike, I just don't think that some of my people believe in my program the way I do."[3]

Months later, however, he agreed to a package of $98 billion in tax increases over three years, while congressional Democrats vowed to cut some $280 billion in spending. Some of his most fervent supporters were aghast. A rising Republican star from New York, Representative Jack Kemp, met with Reagan and begged him to resist the tax hike. "He is adamant that we are wrong on the tax increase," Reagan wrote in his diary. "He is in fact unreasonable. The tax increase is the price we have to pay to get the budget cuts."[4]

The compromise found adversaries Ronald Reagan and House Speaker Tip O'Neill in the same camp, twisting arms in favor of the proposed budget. In mid-August, Reagan made a televised pitch for the budget, tax hikes and all. Several days later, Reagan noted that O'Neill had "made a speech to Republicans telling them why they should support me. It seemed very strange."[5] Equally strange was Reagan's diary notation after the budget passed. He complained about "our ultra pure conservatives" who "deserted" him by voting against the budget.[6] Ironically, these "pure conservatives" were the very people who did believe in his program. It was, after all, the president himself who changed his position.

As if to make up for this bitter compromise, the administration pushed hard for passage of a constitutional amendment requiring the federal government to submit a balanced budget. The annual deficit was projected to break the $100 billion mark within five years (in reality, it rose to more than $200 billion in 1983), a startling figure that shocked the nation and the financial community when the projections were released in midsummer 1982. But the balanced-budget amendment was, in the end, more a symbolic than an actual debate, supported as it was by a president whose own budget was mired in red ink.

In the midst of the summertime budget battle, Nancy Reagan's father, Dr. Loyal Davis, died just a few days after the president sent him a long letter urging him to reconsider his skepticism of religious faith. While Davis did not share Reagan's abiding faith in God, he had been a profound influence on Reagan. He died on August 19, while his son-in-law worked the White House phones in a last-minute effort to get his budget passed.

By October, there were some signs that the economy might be shaking off its doldrums. The Dow Jones Industrial Index rose to over 1,000 and economic growth picked up slightly. But still, the nation's mood was sour, and voters seemed inclined to agree that "Reaganomics" had been a disaster. The president's popularity rating would soon sink below 50 percent.

With midterm elections approaching, Reagan scheduled a prime-time television speech on October 13 to address the country's discontent and to rally Republican troops. Speaking from behind his desk in the Oval Office, dressed as usual in a blue suit, he launched into his speech in a characteristically folksy style. He noted that in "recent days all of us have been swamped by a sea of economic statistics—some good, some bad, and some just plain confusing." It was not hard to picture Americans watching in their living rooms and nodding in agreement. The president seemed to understand what they were thinking. "Behind every one of those numbers are millions of individual lives," he said, "young couples struggling to make ends meet, teenagers looking for work, older Americans threatened by inflation, small businessmen fighting for survival, and parents working for a better future for their children." He knew that many Americans were "desperately trying to make sense out of all the statistics, slogans, and political jargon filling the airwaves in this election year."

Here was yet another example of Reagan's intuitive ability to cast himself as an antipolitician, an outsider who shared his audience's disdain for confusing "political jargon." Never mind that the man was speaking from the Oval Office. The sympathetic words and earnest demeanor made him seem like just another working stiff whose concerns did not square with cold economic analysis or heated political debate over unemployment or inflation rates.

Reagan could talk the talk of the American everyman because, he said, he heard the concerns of America "on visits to schools, meeting halls, factories, and fairgrounds across the country." He wished, he said, that he could share every story he heard, but he decided to choose just one. He read from a letter he received from a woman named Judith from Selma,

Alabama, a woman who, like his audience, couldn't square economic statistics with real life.

Reagan recounted that she wrote to him one morning before dawn because she couldn't sleep. In Selma, she wrote, nearly 19 percent of the city's population was out of work. Those who had jobs had a hard time paying bills. They didn't want a handout. They just wanted to get back on their feet.

"Well, Judith," Reagan said, "I hear you. And millions of other men and women like you stand for the values of hard work, thrift, commitment to family, and love of God that made this country so great and will make us great again." It may have sounded like syrupy pap in Washington, but Reagan was counting on quite a different reception in Selma and places like it.

While Reagan couldn't resist his homily, he was shrewd enough to know that the words would ring hollow if he seemed out of touch with reality, particularly the reality of double-digit unemployment. He conceded that it was "the problem uppermost on many people's minds," and it was a problem he understood from first-hand experience. "I was twenty-one and looking for work in 1932, one of the worst years of the Great Depression," he said. "And I can remember one bleak night in the thirties when my father learned on Christmas Eve that he'd lost his job."

Jack Reagan was a traveling salesman in December 1931, and was doing well enough to expect a bonus for the holidays. Instead, a letter arrived that night via special delivery, informing Jack that he had been fired. Young Ronald Reagan was home from college that night, and he never forgot the trauma of that Christmas Eve. It was his reply to those who accused him of being meanspirited and without compassion.

"To be young in my generation," he said, "was to feel that your future had been mortgaged out from under you, and that's a tragic mistake we must never allow our leaders to make again." But who made the mistakes? Was it Herbert Hoover, the Republican president from 1929 to 1933? Or was it Franklin Roosevelt, the man Reagan supported four times? The president left that question unanswered.

Reagan hauled out a visual aid, a chart with a jagged red line showing the nation's unemployment rate since 1968. Every time unemployment rose, he said, the nation's leaders applied "quick fixes" that led to only short-term relief. He brought out a second chart, this one with a blue line showing the inflation rate zigging and zagging like the unemployment rate, although trending ever upwards. "My fellow Americans," he said, "we've got to stop these trendlines to disaster."

The way to do it, he said, was to avoid the temptation of a quick fix. That was the old way, he said. "Well, at my age I didn't come to Washington to play politics as usual … I came to Washington to try to solve problems, not to sweep them under the rug and leave them for those who will come later."

Reagan as the outsider; Reagan as the average citizen, come to Washington to resolve problems that paralyzed mere politicians. Insiders didn't understand the mystique, this bond between the crusading outsider and his supporters. But Reagan understood it, and communicated it.

Having started his speech by siding with Americans who were confused by a sea of statistics, Reagan now offered a tidal wave of numbers of his own in defense of his economic program. Income tax rates, he noted, had been cut by 25 percent. The rate of government spending growth was down by two-thirds. Inflation had been cut from 12.4 percent in 1980 to 5.1 percent. Interest rates were down to 12 percent. This good news, he said, had been ignored by those who sounded the "drumbeat of doom and gloom" in Washington.

Reagan held out hope that a lame-duck Congress would return to work after Election Day and take up his call to cut government spending more, consider a balanced-budget amendment to the Constitution, further streamline government regulation, and pass low-tax enterprise zones to encourage investment in neglected areas.

The task before America, he said, was "not an easy job." But the nation could no longer afford the solutions of the past because they did nothing to bring about genuine economic reform and hope. "Together," he said, "we've chosen a new road for America. It's a far better road. We need only the courage to see it through.

"We can do it, my fellow Americans, by staying the course."

It was a rousing end to an effective speech, but three weeks later, Americans went to the polls and chose a middle course. While Republicans held onto their fifty-four to forty-six advantage in the Senate, they lost seats in the House, where Democrats added twenty-six seats to their large majority.

Staying the course would prove more difficult than Reagan imagined.

Soviet T–72 tanks travel across Red Square in Moscow

CHAPTER 12

The Evil Empire

Speech to the
National Association of Evangelicals
March 8, 1983

TRACK 12

LTHOUGH HE WAS NOT A FREQUENT CHURCHGOER, AND ALTHOUGH HIS formative years were spent in Hollywood—nobody's idea of a sacred space—Ronald Reagan was a profoundly religious man who was never shy about citing God in his public addresses. He and his predecessor, the born-again Jimmy Carter, helped reshape American political discourse in the late 20th century with their emphasis on personal faith. Americans in the early 21st century have come to take such references for granted, but until Carter and Reagan, it was rare indeed for American presidents to speak of God save for a traditional closing reference to the Almighty in their inaugural addresses.

Evangelical Christianity underwent a revival in the Bible Belt and beyond in the late 1970s and early 1980s. But this movement was more than a latter-day great awakening of faith and practice. Inspired by charismatic preachers who delivered their stirring messages of piety and traditional values on television, millions of Americans, most of them Protestants, joined a loosely organized Christian evangelical movement that sought to make its voice heard not only in the heavens, but in the nation's capital as well.

One of the movement's leaders, the Rev. Jerry Falwell, gave the movement its name: the Moral Majority. Falwell tapped into the cultural resentments that Richard Nixon identified in 1969 when he asked for the support of what he called the great "silent majority" of Americans who, Nixon believed, were put off by disorderly protests and an alien counterculture.

Falwell and other leaders of the burgeoning Christian evangelical movement were unapologetic about mixing faith and politics. Ironically enough, in 1980, they supported Reagan, who was not known for overt displays of piety, over Carter, who wore his religion on his sleeve and who counted himself among the born-again. But Reagan's politics were more in keeping with those of the movement—the evangelicals opposed abortion, sought to return prayer to public schools, and loathed atheistic Soviet Communism as strongly as Reagan did.

The organizational strength of the evangelical movement could be measured, in part, in the national debate over abortion, which many politicians regarded as a settled issue as recently as 1976. But by 1980, as cultural politics took on a new importance, conservative Republicans like Reagan disassociated themselves with the party's previous position. As a result, Reagan captured two-thirds of the evangelical vote in 1980.

Although Reagan criticized abortion as a candidate and then while president, he did little to turn his rhetoric into reality. His first Supreme Court appointment, Sandra Day O'Connor, drew criticism from Falwell and other cultural conservatives because they believed, correctly as it turned out, that she would not vote to overturn *Roe v. Wade*, the 1973 Supreme Court decision that legalized abortion. Senator Barry Goldwater, from O'Connor's home state of Arizona, saw the preacher as an obstructionist, saying that Christians ought to "kick Falwell right in the ass."[1] Goldwater's crusty remarks helped staunch the religious right's criticism, illustrating his new status—thanks to Reagan's victory—as a prophet, not a martyr. But the remark also pointed to the clergyman's power as the leader of a vast new movement based not in political clubhouses, but in churches. Despite misgivings over O'Connor's appointment, the Christian Right was, by 1983, an important part of the new electoral bloc Reagan was building on the remnants of the old Democratic/New Deal coalition. Evangelicals were concerned not only about abortion, but about teenage sex and pregnancy, a perceived breakdown of family life and civil order, gratuitous violence in popular culture and real life, and demands by feminists and, later, gay rights advocates. Reagan was a curious choice as their champion. He was divorced, his family life was complex (his daughter, Patti Davis, was very much a child of the post-1960s), and as a candidate he seemed far more at home with issues of taxation, regulation, and anti-Communism than he was with the kind of cultural criticism that animated his religious supporters.

Nevertheless, evangelicals recognized Reagan as a man with whom they could do business. For there was another issue of deep concern to the movement: the apparent advance, in the 1970s, of Soviet Communism and its godless ethic. Reagan's contempt for Communism appealed to the evangelicals' insistence that the Soviets represented more than simply a competing economic system. They were, in fact, an atheistic, materially driven superpower intent on replacing religious rituals with worship of the state and party. Reagan and the religious right agreed that the Soviet Union was not just bad, not just inefficient, not just repressive, but evil.

Reagan wished to say as much in his speech to the British Parliament in the spring of 1982, however, several advisors insisted that he tone down his remarks, particularly any references to the Soviet Union as "evil." Less than a year later, the president and his chief speechwriter, Anthony Dolan, decided to revisit the topic when Reagan accepted an invitation to speak at the annual convention of the National Association of Evangelicals in March 1983. The meeting of conservative clerics figured to be a far more receptive audience for any discussion of good and evil—topics rarely addressed in the polite language of diplomacy, but a recurring theme among people of faith.

Reagan's more moderate aides, like communications director David Gergen, were less than comfortable with apocalyptic imagery and us versus them rhetoric. When Gergen and others were shown a draft of the speech, they objected to some of its strongest language. But this time, they failed to stop Reagan from being Reagan.

In the months since the president's speech in Britain, the nuclear freeze movement continued to grow in numbers and influence on both sides of the Atlantic. Politicians in the United States were feeling the pressure—in late 1982, the Democratic-controlled House of Representatives declined to fund a new weapons system, the MX missile, estimated to cost $26 billion. The vote did not kill the system; in fact, it was revived with a simple thump to the chest, courtesy of the Senate. But it was clear that the nuclear freeze movement was gaining momentum, much to Reagan's chagrin.

Since the London speech, the Soviet leadership had changed for the first time in nearly two decades. Leonid Brezhnev died in November, after having exchanged several chilly messages with Reagan. The new Soviet leader was Yuri Andropov, a onetime head of the KGB and, at age sixty-eight, a slightly younger man than Reagan.

Although Reagan offered to resume arms-reduction talks with the Soviets and had met privately with the longtime Soviet ambassador to the United States, Anatoly Dobrynin, the attitudes he enunciated in Margaret Thatcher's Britain had not changed. He told the members of Parliament that the West should no longer be shy about stating the truth about the Soviets. As he prepared for his speech in Orlando, he decided to lead by example.

The speech to the evangelical preachers was not billed as a major policy address, and, in any case, the president's audience of twelve hundred clerics was not considered particularly prestigious. The usual White House beat reporters were in attendance, as they always were, but the speech attracted little special attention in advance.

With the leading members of the evangelical group seated on the stage behind him, Reagan launched into what appeared to be a made-to-order address for conservative clergy worried about bread-and-butter cultural issues such as abortion, premarital sex, and a decline in morality. Reagan appealed to their sense of grievance, telling them that the values they stood for—"like concern for others and respect for the rule of law under God"—were under attack by "modern-day secularism." Reagan understood the cultural anxieties of the evangelicals and their supporters, and that came not from cold political calculation, but of his own concerns. When he complained that "no one seems to mention morality as playing a part in the subject of sex," he was not simply playing to the anxieties of his audience. He, too, worried about the lingering effects of the 1960s counterculture he saw firsthand when he was governor of California.

Slowly, paragraph by paragraph, he built an argument not about abortion, not about teenage sex, not even about religion, but about the nature of the Soviet Union. "There is sin and evil in the world," he said, "and we're enjoined by Scripture and the Lord Jesus to oppose it with all our might."

Neutrality in a struggle with evil would not do. The United States was faced with an enemy that believed that morality "is entirely subordinate to the interests of class war." Regrettably, he said, "many influential people" averted their eyes from Communism's basic truths. Such people supported the nuclear freeze movement, unwilling or unable to see that a freeze would benefit the Soviets, and thus, the advocates of godless global Communism. Reagan was appalled that among those who seemed unwilling to stand up to the Soviets were mainstream Protestant, Catholic, and Jewish organizations that offered their moral authority to the growing demand for a freeze in nuclear deployment. With that support, nuclear freeze had moved from the streets to the nation's houses of worship to the halls of Congress: a resolution calling for an immediate freeze in nuclear weaponry had just passed the House Foreign Affairs Committee. Reagan believed the clergy who supported nuclear freeze were not, in fact, making a moral stand. Indeed, they were avoiding one.

A nuclear freeze, he said, "would reward the Soviet Union for its unparalleled military buildup ... And the kind of freeze that has been suggested would be virtually impossible to verify."

To an audience that would have appreciated the reference, Reagan quoted the English author C.S. Lewis, whose works explored Christian themes. Lewis, Reagan said, showed that evil was "conceived and ordered ... in clean, carpeted, warmed and well-lighted offices, by quiet men with white collars and cut fingernails and smooth-shaven cheeks who do not need to raise their voice." History taught that these banal men would never respond to "simple-minded appeasement," no matter how much the naïve might engage in "wishful thinking."

"So," Reagan continued, pausing just for a breath as he moved toward the speech's most remembered passage, "I urge you to speak out against those who would place the United States in a position of military and moral inferiority ... So, in your discussions of the nuclear freeze proposals, I urge you to beware the temptation of pride—the temptation of blithely declaring yourselves above it all and label both sides equally at fault, to ignore the facts of history and the aggressive impulses of an evil empire, to simply call the arms race a giant misunderstanding and thereby remove yourself from the struggle between right and wrong and good and evil."

The evil empire. The phrase would forever be associated with Ronald Reagan and this moment in time, when before an audience of religious evangelicals, the president of the United States condemned the Soviet Union in words never heard before from the leader of the Free World. Soviet Communism had appalled John F. Kennedy no less than Ronald Reagan, but even after viewing the Berlin wall, his nearly unscripted tirade did not present the Cold War in such stark language. Richard Nixon, who made his name as a Communist hunter, nurtured détente as president, viewing the Soviets as negotiating partners, and not as "the focus of evil in the modern world," as Reagan described the Soviet Union elsewhere in his Orlando speech.

In a sense, Reagan said nothing in Orlando that he had not said as a private citizen and as a candidate for president. But presidents did not speak that way.

This one did. And he was not entirely finished. He quoted Whittaker Chambers, the onetime Communist who turned against the party and named Alger Hiss as a Soviet spy. Chambers, Reagan told the clerics, once said that "the crisis of the Western World exists to the degree in which the West is indifferent to God, the degree to which it collaborates in communism's attempt to make man stand alone without God."

The attempt was doomed, he said, as was Communism itself, a "sad, bizarre chapter in human history whose last pages even now are being written."

He concluded his speech with a quote from one of his heroes from the founding era, Thomas Paine, a man known in his time not only as a propagandist for the American Revolution, but as an aggressive critic of religious belief. But, as Reagan noted, Paine believed that "we have within our power to begin the world over again." That power remained in America's grasp, the President added, echoing a sentiment he expressed in his inaugural address.

The president received a rousing ovation, but the applause did not extend to the media. The next day's coverage of what was supposed to be an innocuous speech to a group of ministers was almost uniformly critical. A prominent national columnist found the speech, and no doubt the audience, "primitive." The new Soviet leader, Andropov, accused Reagan of launching a "crusade against socialism as a social system."[2] Historian Henry Steele Commager said the speech was the worst ever given by a president. Ever.

It seemed, for a time, that Reagan might have overplayed his rhetorical cards. Despite his pleas, the U.S. Roman Catholic bishops issued a pastoral letter in support of nuclear freeze several weeks after the Orlando speech. The source was significant, for Reagan had enjoyed the support of millions of nominally Democratic Catholics in 1980. The nuclear freeze movement continued to grow after the speech.

By the end of 1983, new intermediate-range nuclear weapons were deployed in West Germany. The nuclear freeze movement eventually fizzled out, but as years passed, Reagan's description of the Soviet Union began to sound not like the primitive ravings of an irrational old man, but as a moment of insight delivered by a prophet.

Ronald Reagan addresses the annual convention of the National Association of Evangelicals

Ronald Reagan addressing the nation from the Oval Office

CHAPTER 13

Star Wars

Address to the
Nation on Defense and National Security
March 23, 1983

TRACK 13

NO AMERICAN PRESIDENT SINCE JOHN F. KENNEDY SPOKE SO contemptuously of Communism, and with such authentic passion, than Ronald Reagan did. So perhaps it was understandable that critics worried about where the president's rhetoric might lead the nation, and the world. His justification for rearming and his framing of the Cold War as a moral crusade certainly seemed like the words of a man preparing for all-out war.

In fact, however, the prospect of a nuclear conflict horrified Ronald Reagan no less than it did any other American. Early on in his presidency, Reagan asked his military advisors for an estimated body count in the event of a nuclear exchange with the Soviets. The Pentagon came back with an estimate of one hundred and fifty million dead Americans. Reagan was appalled. He wrote: "My dream, then, became a world free of nuclear weapons."[1]

Reagan despised the philosophical underpinning of nuclear deterrence—the concept of mutually assured destruction, known better by its chillingly appropriate acronym, MAD. The MAD doctrine had it that neither the United States nor the Soviet Union would dare attempt a nuclear first strike because such an attack would only provoke a response in kind, leading to the destruction of both nations and a fair portion of the globe.

MAD was a horrifying but utterly pragmatic calculation in a world that lived on the edge of unparalleled catastrophe. It sounded mad, indeed, and perhaps it was. But pragmatists in both nations were quick to point out one salient fact: MAD worked. Neither the Soviet Union nor the United States had ever fired a nuclear shot in anger at each other, despite tensions and competition that surely would have led to war in another, less scientifically advanced, era.

For Ronald Reagan, however, MAD was insane. He came to that conclusion long before he won the presidency and with it command of the nation's formidable nuclear arsenal. MAD, he wrote in his autobiography, "didn't seem to me to be something that would send you to bed feeling safe. It was like having two westerners standing in a saloon aiming their guns at each other's head—permanently. There had to be a better way."[2]

Reagan was not the first president to wish for some better way. Negotiations designed to limit the growth of nuclear weaponry—and hopefully reduce the chances of nuclear war—were a regular feature of U.S.-Soviet relations since John Kennedy proposed a ban on testing nuclear weapons in the atmosphere in 1963. Arms control talks had their successes and their failures, but MAD remained a central tenet of nuclear strategy. Neither side had any reason to give up on MAD, because in its chilling rationality, it had in fact prevented the Cold War from becoming the ultimate and final world war.

Reagan refused to accept the cold-blooded calculation that was at the heart of MAD. If the public saw him as a bellicose Cold War cowboy, privately, he was anything but. He loathed the gruesome language that some of his more-hawkish advisors used when discussing weapons of mass destruction. "They tossed around macabre jargon about 'throw weights' and 'kill ratios' as if they were talking about baseball scores," Reagan wrote.[3] Nuclear weapons were designed to slaughter civilians, and Reagan had little patience with advisors who insisted that nuclear exchanges would involve only military targets.

That impatience—with arms-control professionals, with advisors seemingly far too willing to consider nuclear war as just another option, with a status quo he found repugnant and immoral—gave birth to one of the Reagan administration's most controversial and surely most innovative ideas, the Strategic Defense Initiative.

Instantly criticized as a science-fiction fantasy worthy of a man from Hollywood—the label of "Star Wars" was not meant as a compliment—SDI was and remains a contested program. Simply put, if anything so complex can be so reduced, Reagan wished to design and deploy a platform in space that could shoot down nuclear-armed ballistic missiles before they reached their targets. Such a shield would make nuclear missiles obsolete, and would make his vision of a world free of nuclear missiles a reality.

It did not occur to Reagan, nor would it, that America was incapable of producing such a complicated piece of technology. From his days as a spokesman for GE, biographer Lou Cannon wrote, Reagan believed in the power of old-fashioned American ingenuity, whether in the cause of making life better for housewives or in reducing the chances of nuclear war. "God gave angels wings," Reagan said in early 1983. "He gave mankind dreams. And with His help, there's no limit to what can be accomplished." Cannon argued that Reagan's faith in Star Wars came out of this faith in God.[4]

But even as Reagan spoke privately about reducing and perhaps even eliminating nuclear weaponry, he continued to move forward with plans to deploy intermediate-range nuclear missiles in Europe to counter a new generation of Soviet missiles. If the goals seemed wildly contradictory, they were not, at least not in Reagan's worldview. He regarded the U.S. buildup as a justifiable reaction to the Soviets' deployment of SS-20 intermediate missiles, but more to the point, he insisted that by countering the SS-20s, the United States would force the Soviets to the bargaining table. There, the two sides could talk about not just a temporary reduction in the growth of nuclear weapons, but actual reductions in nuclear stockpiles. Otherwise, he said, the Soviets had no incentive to talk.

Reagan himself had been talking about arms reduction since 1976, during his failed campaign to wrest the Republican Party's presidential nomination from Gerald Ford. At a time when the United States and Soviets were engaged in negotiations to limit nuclear weapons—the Strategic Arms Limitation Talks—Reagan told aides that he favored not limitations, but outright reductions. One of those aides, Martin Anderson, later admitted, "Nobody believed there was the slightest possibility it could happen. And when Reagan began to talk privately of a dream he had when someday we might live in a world free of all nuclear missiles, well, we just smiled."[5]

Three years later, Anderson accompanied Reagan on a tour of the North American Aerospace Defense Command buried deep within the mountains of Colorado. NORAD was a bunker on steroids, a huge, windowless complex of offices, consoles, and computer screens where a small army watched and waited for signs of an incoming nuclear missile. In the event of an imminent attack, NORAD would provide Washington with the information it would require before launching a counterstrike. According to Anderson, Reagan asked NORAD's commander, Air Force General James Hill, what would happen if the Soviets launched a single missile at a single American city. Hill replied that the target would have about ten or fifteen minutes notice. "That's all we can do," Hill told Reagan. "We can't stop it."[6]

After the tour, as the two visitors flew back to California, a somber Reagan told Anderson that the United States "should have some way of defending ourselves against nuclear weapons."[7] Reagan's aides began researching, quietly, the possibilities for a missile defense system. Few people noticed that at the Republican National Convention in 1980, when Reagan was nominated for the presidency, the party called for the development of an antiballistic missile system—even though the Anti-Ballistic Missile Treaty of 1972 explicitly banned such a system.

Reagan said nothing about missile defense during the 1980 campaign, but as soon as he was elected, his top advisors began investigating its feasibility. In early February 1983, Reagan met with members of the Joint Chiefs of Staff—his top military commanders—and several cabinet members. During the session, missile defense came up for discussion, prompted by the president's almost wistful inquiry into its feasibility at a previous meeting. Admiral James Watkins told Reagan that development of a missile defense system was "possibly within reach."[8]

That was all Reagan needed to hear. The military commanders did not explicitly endorse the idea of a missile defense system, and they certainly did not say that the United States had the technology in place to begin creating, never mind building and deploying, such a system. They certainly did not mean to suggest that MAD was destined to join Communism—to adopt Reagan's view—on the ash heap of history.

Those were details—important details, but details all the same. And details were not Reagan's strong suit, as even his admirers would admit. In any case, the nation didn't need to know details. What they needed was a vision, and Ronald Reagan, nuclear abolitionist, was ready to offer one.

The president could barely contain his enthusiasm in the weeks after his meeting with the Joint Chiefs. He already was scheduled to give a prime-time speech to the nation on March 23 about defense spending. He decided to use that opportunity to talk about his vision of a world where nuclear missiles were rendered obsolete, a world in which phrases like "throw weights" and "kill ratios" would no longer conjure nightmares of a world gone mad.

Reagan and a handful of aides decided he would mention missile defense at the conclusion of a speech devoted, ironically enough, to his military buildup, including the U.S. deployment of intermediate nuclear missiles in Europe. McFarlane, who saw missile defense merely as a shiny chit to play at the arms-control bargaining table, wrote several paragraphs describing the concept—with Reagan adding language of his own to the draft—tacked it onto the end of the speech, and circulated it to the Joint Chiefs just three days before air time. They were astonished to realize that Reagan was ready to go public with an idea that was, in their view, in the earliest stages of discussion and debate. Even more surprised were Reagan's secretaries of defense and state, along with their top aides. They found out about the speech on the morning it was to be delivered. They were aghast, but there was little they could do.

The president began his speech at 8:02 p.m., Washington time, from the Oval Office. There was little to indicate any special urgency to his message beyond the political give-and-take of the moment. The White House and Capitol Hill had been sparring over military spending since Day One of Reagan's presidency, and by the early spring of 1983, the American public had heard many of these arguments before. Reagan warned that "liberals in the House of Representatives" were trying to cut "our defense spending by $163 billion over the next five years." Such cuts, he argued, would lead to "greater risk" of war or a reduction in "our commitments" to allies. "We maintain the peace through our strength; weakness only invites aggression."

And Reagan found evidence of aggression around the world, which he took as a sign that the Soviets were not certain about America's commitment to strengthening its defenses. In addition to their buildup of conventional and nuclear forces, the Soviets were engaged in intrigue "very close to home: Central America and the Caribbean Basin."

Reagan displayed a series of photographs showing what he said was evidence of a huge Soviet buildup on Cuba, that eternal pebble in Uncle Sam's shoe. America was, of course, familiar with a Soviet military presence ninety miles off the Florida coast. But Reagan also saw a growing threat on another island, one few Americans had heard of: Grenada. He noted the presence of Cuban workers and engineers on the island, a former British colony, and their contribution to the construction of an airport with a huge, ten-thousand-foot runway. "Grenada doesn't even have an air force," Reagan noted. "Who is it intended for?" Somebody, he implied, who would be interested in disrupting oil shipments bound for the United States.

From the Caribbean to Ethiopia to Afghanistan to Poland, the Soviets were flexing the muscles they'd been developing for a decade or more. The United States had little choice but to respond to muscle with a display of its own—an expensive display. On his shopping list were a new long-range bomber, the B-1, a six hundred ship Navy (up from fewer than five hundred vessels), and new submarines.

Necessary though these measures were, they were not satisfying. Nor were conventional negotiations designed to limit nuclear arms because in the end, "it will still be necessary to rely on the specter of retaliation, on mutual threat. And that's a sad commentary on the human condition."

Reagan's expression did not change as he set the stage for his startling proposal. "Let me share with you a vision of the future which offers hope," he said. "What if free people could live secure in the knowledge that their security did not rest upon the threat of instant U.S. retaliation to deter a Soviet attack, that we could intercept and destroy strategic ballistic missiles before they reached our own soil or that of our allies?"

In the embassies of Washington DC, from the newsrooms of the nation's elite media organizations, and from the homes of some high-ranking members of the administration a thousand eyebrows were raised and a thousand voices asked the same question: "Did he just say what I think he said?"

He had, indeed.

"I know this is a formidable, technical task, one that may not be accomplished before the end of this century," he said in a marvelous piece of understatement. "Yet, current technology has attained a level of sophistication where it's reasonable for us to begin this effort. It will take years, probably decades of effort on many fronts … But isn't it worth every investment necessary to free the world from the threat of nuclear war? We know it is."

Reagan's only concession to the professional arms-control community was a pledge that any work carried out on missile defense would be done in accordance with the Anti-Ballistic Missile treaty. But that was a detail that required no more than a routine disclaimer. Reagan wanted to focus not on details, but on a vision—his vision.

"I call upon the scientific community in our country," he said, "those who gave us nuclear weapons, to turn their great talents now to the cause of mankind and world peace, to give us the means of rendering these nuclear weapons impotent and obsolete." Redemption was at hand; those who showed how to destroy the world could now show how to make the world safe, safe from destruction, safe from the dark side of science.

There was no question in Reagan's mind that a great moment was at hand.

"My fellow Americans, tonight we're launching an effort which holds the promise of changing the course of human history," he said as he concluded. "There will be risks, and results take time. But I believe we can do it."

He was nearly alone in that assessment, based on the following day's media accounts. Newspapers almost uniformly described his vision as little more than a fantasy, a plan cooked up by a man who had watched (or starred in?) too many science fiction movies. More pragmatically, critics asserted that Reagan wished to distract the public's attention from the huge cost of his buildup, although it wasn't clear how he would achieve that goal by unveiling another expensive program.

More than two decades have passed since Ronald Reagan publicly proposed a missile shield. Billions of dollars have been spent on research and development, but the dream seems as elusive as ever.

If nothing else, though, Reagan's bold speech underscored his impatience with a doctrine called MAD, and with those who believed there was no alternative to it.

Cuban President Fidel Castro talks with Nicaraguan President Daniel Ortega

CHAPTER 14

The Challenge of Central America

Speech to a
Joint Session of Congress
April 27, 1983

TRACK 14

URING WORLD WAR II, WINSTON CHURCHILL ARGUED AGAINST A DIRECT confrontation with Nazi Germany's Fortress Europe—a massive series of defensive installations along the coast of France and the Low Countries. Instead, he said, the Allies should concentrate their strategy and resources on what he called the "underbelly" of Nazi-occupied Europe: North Africa, Italy, and the Balkan states. Churchill believed the Allies would have an easier time attacking Germany from the south, rather than from the west.

Ronald Reagan believed that when the Soviets looked at a map of the United States, they saw Central America in the same way that Churchill saw Italy and the Balkans—as a soft, vulnerable, and inviting target. A blow there could inflict maximum damage with minimal cost.

Reagan was haunted, consciously or not, by another precedent: the Communist victory in China in 1949. "Who lost China?" had been a rallying cry for conservative anti-Communists who believed that the Truman administration's lack of resolve led to Mae Ze-dong's victory. With the Marxist Sandinistas in power in Nicaragua and a leftist guerilla movement challenging a corrupt and oppressive government in neighboring El Salvador, Ronald Reagan feared that inaction might lead Americans one day to ask, "Who lost Central America?" In early 1983, he confided to his diary that if the United States did not increase its aid to the government in El Salvador, "We're going to lose this one."[1]

Reagan's anxieties about Central America seemed to contradict his confident assertion, made in Britain in 1982, that Marxism-Leninism was destined for the ash heap of history. What's more, his adamant support for the government of El Salvador surely seemed at odds with his steadfast belief in democracy, liberty, and freedom. The regime and its supporters routinely murdered civilians, including priests and nuns. Catholic Archbishop Oscar Romero and four American churchwomen were among the victims of pro-government death squads. Reagan was aware of the brutality, but nevertheless insisted that the United States provide military aid against rebels who were supported by Cuba and the Sandinistas in Nicaragua, who themselves were battling a U.S.-supported rebel movement known as the Contras.

Under Reagan, the whole of Central America became a theater of operations designed to prevent a new domino effect, this one much closer to home. Two decades earlier, fears that a Communist takeover of South Vietnam would lead to the collapse of other governments in Southeast Asia had led the Kennedy and Johnson administrations to commit hundreds of thousands of troops in a vain effort to stop a Communist insurgency. Now, in Reagan's view, Communist guerillas were in America's backyard, with the support of Cuba and the Soviet Union. That was reason enough to back anti-Communist leaders, no matter how dubious. In Guatemala, where leftist rebels were challenging another oppressive government, Reagan gave his full support to President José Efraín Ríos Montt, a murderous dictator whose army was responsible for the slaughter of thousands of civilians. Reagan met with Ríos Montt in late 1982, praised him publicly, and offered to assist him with military hardware.

Getting Ríos Montt that assistance—in fact, implementing Reagan's overall strategy in Central America—was no simple matter. Congressional Democrats, particularly the leaders in the House of Representatives, did not share Reagan's alarmist view of the region's violent instability and were infuriated to learn that the United States was covertly financing and training anti-Sandinista guerillas in Honduras. Beginning in 1982, Rep. Edward Boland of Massachusetts authored a series of amendments designed to cut off American financial support for the Contras' military campaign against the Sandinistas. The Reagan administration resented what it saw as congressional interference in the conduct of foreign affairs. During Reagan's second term, the White House would circumvent the Boland Amendment, with disastrous results.

William Casey, director of the Central Intelligence Agency, and other administration officials continued to argue that Central America represented a clear and present danger to American national security. But historian John Patrick Diggins noted, two decades later, that the Soviets were not especially interested in the region, although they surely did not mind any trouble that the Sandinistas or others might cause the United States. In fact, Diggins wrote, Fidel Castro was angry that the Soviets did not wish to play a more active role in supporting antigovernment guerillas in El Salvador.[2] Reagan's own advisors were divided on the topic. Some were willing to drop the campaign against the Sandinistas if the Sandinistas agreed to stop their support for the rebels in El Salvador. Others believed the Sandinistas ought to be crushed along with the Salvadoran rebels. In spring 1982, Secretary of State Alexander Haig pushed for military blockade of Cuba to stop the flow of arms from Castro to Nicaragua. Over the longer term, aides such as Jeanne Kirkpatrick, Reagan's ambassador to the UN, and Bud McFarlane, assistant national security advisor, thought no military solution was possible without social reform in the area. But hardliners insisted that only the destruction of Marxist insurgencies would stabilize the area.

In the spring of 1983, with House Democrats continuing to raise rhetorical and legislative objections to his Central American policy, Reagan decided to bring his case directly to Capitol Hill and the people. Many of his aides thought it unwise to expend political capital in such a public way—to a joint session of Congress and before a national television audience. The president, however, insisted. He had taken on Congress before and lived to tell the tale. He would attempt to do so again.

Just after eight o'clock in Washington, on the evening of April 27, House Speaker Tip O'Neill introduced the president to the senators and representatives gathered in the House chamber. O'Neill and Reagan already had had many disagreements since Inauguration Day, 1981, but they managed to retain affection for each other. O'Neill, though, was close to Boland, author of the legislation that Reagan believed tied his hands in dealing with the Sandinistas. "They began battling to limit virtually everything the administration was trying to do in Central America," Reagan wrote of O'Neill and Boland.3 During a meeting between Reagan and O'Neill about Central America, the president lost his temper, a rare occurrence. The president snarled: "The Sandinistas have openly proclaimed Communism in their country and their support of Marxist revolutions throughout Central America … they're killing and torturing people! Now what the hell does Congress expect me to do about that?"4

On April 27, he proposed to tell Congress what he planned to do about it.

Reagan made it clear that he believed the stakes were high, and that bipartisan cooperation was needed to prevent a crisis south of the border. Central America, he noted, "is much closer to the United States than many of the world trouble spots that concern us … El Salvador is nearer to Texas than Texas is to Massachusetts. Nicaragua is just as close to Miami, San Antonio, San Diego, and Tucson as those cities are to Washington," he said, driving home a point intended not so much for the members of Congress but for those watching at home who might wonder why the president seemed so concerned about small countries about which most Americans knew little.

Their disinterest in the region, Reagan said, was a mistake. "If the Nazis during World War II and the Soviets today could recognize the Caribbean and Central America as vital to our interests, shouldn't we, also? For several years now, under two administrations, the United States has been increasing its defense of freedom in the Caribbean Basin. And I can tell you tonight, democracy is beginning to take root in El Salvador, which, until a short time ago, knew only dictatorship."

Reagan's assertion about El Salvador was, at best, wishful thinking. But his reference to the efforts of "two administrations" was strategic. In trying to bridge the partisan divide over Central American policy, Reagan hoped to remind Democrats that the Carter administration "did not hesitate," as he said later in his speech, to arm the government of El Salvador. But Reagan's mention of Carter probably did not prompt the sort of reaction the president was hoping for from O'Neill and his allies. Their relationship with Carter was tepid at best.

Reagan continued to make the case that El Salvador was indeed making progress towards democracy, and paid tribute to anonymous Salvadorans who voted in a national election a month earlier—an election the rebel movement had boycotted. He told of a woman who was threatened with death for going to the polls. Reagan said, "She told the guerillas, 'You can kill me, you can kill my family, you can kill my neighbors. You can't kill us all.'" Such people, he said, were the true "freedom fighters" in El Salvador, not the rebels who "were exposed for what they really are—a small minority who want power for themselves and their backers, not democracy for the people."

Moving to Nicaragua, Reagan asserted that the United States had tried to be friendly and supportive of the Sandinista government, but it had "treated us like an enemy." He insisted that the rebels who were trying to overthrow the government in Nicaragua were not allies of the discredited dictator Anastasio Somoza, whom the Sandinistas had overthrown in 1979, but were, in fact, "anti-Somoza heroes" who were fighting "because they truly wanted democracy for Nicaragua and they still do." Reagan's use of the word "heroes" to describe the anti-Somoza opponents of the Sandinistas was ironic, for in the past, the U.S. government had famously supported the Somoza regime against such heroic resistance.

Adopting a defensive tone, Reagan insisted that his administration did not seek to overthrow the Sandinistas, but he also said that the United States "should not, and we will not, protect the Nicaraguan government from the anger of its own people."

After justifying his policies in the region, Reagan turned to another Democrat, Harry Truman, who in 1947 spoke before a joint session of Congress to pledge American support for the war-torn nations of Europe who were trying to resist the pressure of Communist insurgencies or infiltration. The outline of that speech, which Reagan quoted extensively, became known as the Truman Doctrine

Reagan used the Truman formula to introduce a similar program in Central America. "Some people have forgotten the successes of those years and the decades of peace, prosperity, and freedom they secured," Reagan said by way of a tribute to the Truman Doctrine. "Some people talk as though the United States were incapable of acting effectively in international affairs without risking war or damaging those we seek to help."

His audience listened intently but skeptically, interrupting Reagan with applause only a handful of times. Republicans led the applause when Reagan said he was sure that Congress would not support "passivity, resignation, defeatism in the face of this challenge to freedom and security in our own hemisphere." Democrats, on the other hand, were quick to cheer Reagan's assurance that "there is no thought of sending American combat troops to Central America. They are not needed."

Conscious of such divisions, Reagan asked for bipartisan support for a four-point program which he hoped would counter such negative talk about the effectiveness of U.S. foreign policy. He first addressed issues of social inequality and economic development, rather than the military effort to contain what he saw as Communist expansion in the region. "First," he said, "we will support democracy, reform, and human freedom ... Second ... we will support economic development ... Our goal must be to focus our immense and growing technology to enhance health care, agriculture, industry, and to ensure that we who inhabit this interdependent region come to know and understand each other better, retaining our diverse identities, respecting our diverse traditions and institutions."

Those two measures, however, were not enough to deal with what Reagan saw as an aggressive military threat to the region. In response "to the military challenge from Cuba and Nicaragua—to their deliberate use of force to spread tyranny—we will support the security of the region's threatened nations," he said. "No amount of reform," he asserted, "will bring peace so long as guerillas believe they will win by force. No amount of economic help will suffice if guerilla units can destroy roads and bridges and power stations and crops, again and again, with impunity."

Finally, he pledged his support for "dialogue and negotiations both among the countries of the region and within each country."

"We want to help opposition groups join the political process in all countries and compete by ballots instead of bullets."

As he neared the end of a thirty-eight minute presentation, Reagan made it clear that he regarded Central America not as a sideshow but as a staging area for direct confrontation with Communism. "The national security of all the Americas is at stake in Central America," he said. "If we cannot defend ourselves there, we cannot expect to prevail elsewhere ... This is not a partisan issue. It is a question of our meeting our moral responsibility to ourselves, our friends and our posterity."

Reagan left the House chamber to cheers, as was customary for any president who visited Capitol Hill for such an occasion. But if he hoped those cheers signaled the bipartisan consensus he hoped he would achieve, he was wrong. Central America remained a contentious issue to the end of his administration, although there was a moment of bipartisan consensus when both Republican Senator Barry Goldwater and Democratic Senator Daniel Patrick Moynihan jointly protested the administration's secret mining of Nicaragua's harbors. Reagan's continued interest in the region and his determination to bring down the Sandinistas would lead to a second-term scandal—Iran-Contra—that tarnished his reputation and led to criminal charges against some of his top aides.

Ronald Reagan meets with CIA Director William Casey in the Oval Office

Cardboard tombstones stand across the street from the White House, memorializing the loss of KAL 007

CHAPTER 15

The Downing of KAL 007

Address to the Nation
September 5, 1983

TRACK 15

D URING THE LONG TWILIGHT STRUGGLE KNOWN AS THE COLD WAR, THE world's greatest fear—one shared by Ronald Reagan—was that a catastrophic misunderstanding or single inflammatory action might set off a chain of events leading to a nuclear holocaust. The Cuban missile crisis of 1962 came close to realizing those terrible fears, but a combination of American military display and back-channel negotiations with Moscow helped bring the standoff to an end.

For some contemporary observers in the early 1980s, the downing of Korean Airlines Flight 007 on the night of August 31, 1983, was another such perilous moment. But that fearful belief was based on a false impression of Ronald Reagan. Those who saw him as reckless and reflexive assumed that the cowboy president would be eager to seize upon the incident as a justification for war with the Soviet Union.

In fact, just as the Cuban Missile Crisis showed that the Kennedy administration was not a prisoner to extreme anti-Communist rhetoric, the downing of KAL 007 demonstrated that President Reagan was not the trigger-happy Cold Warrior his critics believed him to be. The tragedy unfolded at a time of heightened tensions between the two superpowers. Secretary of State Alexander Haig had resigned abruptly in June 1982, to be replaced by George

Shultz. Reagan's two hard-line anti-Soviet speeches, the first to the British Parliament, the second to the American evangelicals in Florida, sent an unmistakable message to Moscow and the rest of the world: the days of détente and accommodation were over. The Soviets certainly got the message, and they responded in kind and in language designed to encourage other nations to believe that Reagan was destroying a comfortable status quo in the Cold War and replacing it with direct confrontation. In one of his last speeches, given two weeks before his death, Soviet leader Leonid Brezhnev accused Reagan of pushing "the world into the flames of nuclear war."[1]

All it would take, many thought, was a spark.

On the night of August 31, 1983, a Korean Airlines 747 took off from Anchorage, Alaska, and began its long journey over the Pacific Ocean toward Seoul, capital of South Korea. The flight had originated in New York City, and among its 269 passengers was a Democratic congressman from Georgia, Lawrence McDonald, whose anti-Soviet speeches were far more extreme than Reagan's. McDonald, a physician by training, was the head of the national John Birch Society, a far-out, right-wing political organization that had once condemned Dwight Eisenhower as an agent of the international Communist conspiracy. McDonald was headed to South Korea to take part in ceremonies commemorating the thirtieth anniversary of a U.S.-South Korea mutual defense treaty, signed after the end of the Korean War.

Several hours into the flight, KAL 007 wandered into Soviet air space over the Kamchatka Peninsula northeast of Japan. Several Soviet fighter planes scrambled and tracked the airliner as it continued to fly off-course, apparently the result of a computer error. After about two and a half hours, one of the Soviet pilots reported that he was in visual contact with the passenger jet. He carried on a methodical conversation with his radio tower as he zeroed in on the 747 and then fired two missiles. A huge burst of fire lit up the sky over the North Pacific. "The target is destroyed," the pilot reported.

Ronald Reagan received word of the attack just after 7:00 a.m. on September 1. The president was in California, but after learning of the disaster, he flew immediately to Washington for a series of meetings with his national security and defense aides. The Soviets at first denied that they were responsible for the attack, but U.S. intelligence had intercepted the conversations between Soviet fighter pilots and their control tower, and Reagan had the tapes.

The president was outraged. He called the attack a massacre and summoned congressional leaders to the White House on the Sunday of Labor Day weekend to brief them on the shoot-down and to play tape recordings of the intercepted communications between the Soviet fighter pilot and his radio tower. The president wanted the legislative leaders to understand what had happened, so they would also understand why he was determined to punish the Soviets.

Secretary Shultz declared that the shoot-down was not just another Cold War issue between the United States and the Soviets. It was, he said, an issue of the Soviets "versus the world."[2] The White House had evidence and moral force on its side, and was determined to make the best use of both.

If the situation was not as fraught as the Cuban missile crisis, it certainly was close. Reagan's allies in the press and in public life called for retaliation. Foreign diplomats and leaders called for calm. On Labor Day, Reagan sat beside the White House swimming pool in a damp swim suit, paper and pen in hand. He had in front of him a draft of a speech worked up by his speechwriting team over the weekend and scheduled for delivery to a national television audience at eight o'clock in the evening, Washington time. He read the draft and was not satisfied. He wanted to "give my unvarnished opinion of the barbarous act," but the draft, he felt, didn't reflect his anger.[3] He also wanted his speech to include portions of the tape recording he had played for congressional leaders. Americans, he decided, ought to hear the evidence themselves. When they did, he was confident they would share his outrage and support whatever actions he might propose.

Reagan inserted the word "massacre" into the final draft of the speech and made several other changes. But for all of his strong rhetoric, the president was not contemplating anything close to war. He told advisors that it was imperative to avoid an overreaction—not the sort of advice his detractors, or, for that matter, some of his strongest supporters, would have anticipated.

Later that evening, Reagan changed from his swim trunks to his usual blue suit, strode into the Oval Office, and shared his rage with an anxious world. He wasted no time in getting to his point. "I'm coming before you tonight about the Korean airline massacre," he began. "This crime against humanity must never be forgotten, here or throughout the world."

"Let me state as plainly as I can: There was absolutely no justification, either legal or moral, for what the Soviets did," he said. "One newspaper in

India said, 'If every passenger plane … is fair game for home air forces … it will be the end to civil aviation as we know it.'"

At a time of growing unease over Washington's more militant stand against the Soviets, when the nuclear freeze movement was gaining support in European capitals and in the United States as well, Reagan at last had world opinion on his side, and he made great use of it. The reference to the Indian newspaper was a deft touch, for India was a nonaligned country. Criticism from India reminded Americans that this was not, as Secretary Shultz said, an issue pitting Americans against the Soviets. This time, Moscow was pitted against world opinion.

But Moscow was admitting nothing, a fact Reagan noted with contempt. Despite the evidence, he said, the Soviets "persistently refused to admit that their pilot fired on the Korean aircraft. Indeed, they've not even told their own people that a plane was shot down."

Reagan took his audience on a step-by-step verbal re-creation of what happened on that moonlit night near the Sea of Japan. He duly noted that earlier that night, KAL 007 and an American reconnaissance airplane were in the same vicinity over international waters. But the U.S. plane was long gone when KAL 007 ventured into Soviet air space.

The Russians tracked the Korean aircraft for two and a half hours, he said, building an argument that the Soviet air command and the fighter pilots must have known that they were stalking a commercial jetliner, not a military plane. As he presented his case, Reagan introduced the tape recordings of the conversations between the fighter pilot and his radio tower. The voices spoke in Russian; an English translation appeared on viewers' screens. As the recording reached its climax, the viewing audience read the final, fatal words: "The target is destroyed."

"Let me point something out here having to do with [the pilot's] close-up view of the airliner, on what we know was a clear night with a half moon," he said. "The 747 has a unique and distinctive silhouette, unlike any other plane in the world. There is no way a pilot could mistake this for anything other than a civilian airliner." A trained fighter pilot surely would know the difference between a 747 and the RC-135 U.S. reconnaissance airplane that had been in the vicinity—but not, Reagan emphasized, over Soviet air space—hours earlier.

The Soviets owed the world an apology, he said, but they continued to "deny the deed." As Reagan's audience watched and listened, at home and around the world, the thought must have crossed many minds: what was he leading to? He called the shoot-down an "atrocity" and a "crime." He compared the shoot-down with the "inhuman brutality" the Soviets had demonstrated in their suppression of revolts in Czechoslovakia in 1968, Hungary in 1956, and Poland in 1981. He accused the Soviets of using poison gas in the "villages of Afghanistan," where the Red Army was fighting an Islamic guerilla movement financed, in part, by an obscure Saudi named Osama bin Laden.

The rhetorical and moral stage was set for a dramatic U.S. reaction. But Reagan was not prepared to go to battle stations. He wished to vent, to use the evidence he had to influence public opinion. But he was not ready to go to war.

Instead, he proposed a series of economic and diplomatic sanctions against the Soviets. Bilateral negotiations were to be suspended. International investigations were requested. Reagan asked Congress to formally condemn the attack. Secretary Shultz would confront the Soviet foreign minister with "our demands for disclosure of the facts." The United States would demand reparations to the families of those killed.

It was, in fact, a measured response to an international crisis. Reagan spared no invective, but he ordered no meaningful retaliation. After his speech, media commentators seemed relieved to note that Reagan's tough talk was not matched by provocative actions. The world breathed a sigh of relief. Perhaps Ronald Reagan was not such a cowboy after all. Surely no cowboy would walk away from such a provocation.

About a month after the KAL shoot-down, Ronald Reagan screened an advance copy of a made-for-TV movie scheduled to be shown in November on ABC. The film, called *The Day After*, was a dramatic and effective depiction of life in Lawrence, Kansas, after a Soviet nuclear attack. Reagan noted in his diary that the film, which dovetailed with demands for a nuclear freeze, was "powerfully done" and left him "greatly depressed."[4]

Fresh from a confrontation with what he saw as Soviet barbarity, Reagan watched the dramatic depiction of nuclear holocaust with special attention. Several days later, he received a briefing from his military advisors about the aftereffects of a real nuclear attack.

The world, he wrote, needed a better "defense against nuclear missiles." And he was determined to find one.[5]

The Soviets continued to blame the United States for the loss of innocent life, insisting that their pilots could not have known the plane was a
civilian craft and that the Central Intelligence Agency was somehow
responsible for the flight's venture into Russian air space. Those accusations
have spawned a cottage industry of conspiracy theories in the years since the
shoot-down. Regardless of which version of the night's events one believes,
there is little question that KAL 007 led to an increase in Soviet-American
tensions at a time when Reagan was intent on a more confrontational East-
West policy.

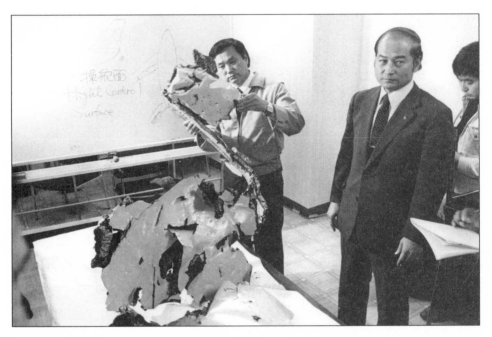

Korean Airlines personnel examine aircraft debris at a Japanese police station

The Reagans honor the victims of the bombing of the U.S. Embassy in Beirut, Lebanon

CHAPTER 16

Terrorism and Triumph

Address on
Lebanon and Grenada
October 27, 1983

TRACK 16

IN THE PREDAWN HOURS OF OCTOBER 25, A U.S. NAVAL TASK FORCE MOVED undetected through the darkness of the South Atlantic, headed for the small island nation of Grenada in the Caribbean. Aboard the ships were members of the 22nd Marine Amphibious Unit, the main contingent of a small invasion force that was about to launch the largest American military action since the Vietnam War.

As the marines gathered themselves for action, some of them about to face hostile fire for the first time in their lives, they had little time to reflect on the disaster that had taken the lives of nearly two hundred and fifty of their comrades half a world away, in Beirut, just two days earlier. Just before six-thirty on Sunday morning, October 23, a suicide bomber driving a truck packed with explosives smashed into a four-story building housing nearly four hundred marines who had been thrust in the middle of a catastrophic civil and regional war in Lebanon. The explosion brought down the building and snuffed out the lives of 241 U.S. soldiers. A similar attack that day killed fifty French soldiers who, like the marines, were part of a multinational armed force attempting to keep peace among Lebanon's warring factions and armies.

The Reagan administration had been criticized for failing to explain what national interest was served by putting American troops at risk in an incomprehensible and multilateral war involving private militias, terrorist cells, as well as elements of the Lebanese, Israeli, and Syrian armed forces. Voices in Congress asked, even before the attacks, why marines were being put in what seemed like an untenable position with no well-defined mission.

Now, as troops and emergency personnel combed the wreckage of the ruined barracks, looking for bodies as well as survivors, another group of marines was headed to battle. But this time, surprise was on their side.

The bombing of the Marine barracks and the invasion of Grenada, where other Marxists had overthrown a Cuban-supported Marxist regime, were among the most dramatic events of the Reagan administration. Critics and skeptics would charge that the events were not unrelated, that Reagan ordered the invasion to distract the public from the disaster in Lebanon, but orders were given before the bombing.

While on a short golfing vacation at the famed Augusta National Golf Club in Georgia, President Reagan was awakened on the morning of October 21 by a phone call from his new national security advisor, Robert "Bud" McFarlane. McFarlane told the president that a group of nations in the Caribbean region, concerned about a bloody coup in Grenada, had called on the United States to intervene. Dressed in a bathrobe and his pajamas, Reagan later met with McFarlane and Secretary of State Shultz and gave his approval for a quick, secret assault on the island, which was home to nearly a thousand American medical students. Reagan went back to sleep, and later that day played a round of golf, had dinner, and retired earlier than usual. He was awakened again by a phone call from McFarlane, this one at two-thirty in the morning. McFarlane broke the news of the attack on the Marine barracks.

Reagan believed there was a connection between the bombing in Lebanon and the coup in Grenada that prompted the U.S. invasion. Speaking to a national television audience from the Oval Office on October 27, he grimly told the American people, "Moscow assisted and encouraged the violence in both countries." But violence in Lebanon appeared to require little assistance or encouragement from outsiders. A civil war that broke out in 1975 had by 1983 led to the deaths of nearly a hundred thousand people and turned one of the Middle East's most-charming cities, Beirut, into a symbol of mindless hatred and inhumanity. Christian and Muslim militias fought each other with uncommon ferocity; Syria shelled

Christian areas to prevent a feared alliance between Christian militias and Israel; and the Israeli warplanes bombed PLO headquarters in Beirut. In June 1982, while Reagan was in Europe, Israel invaded southern Lebanon and sent its warplanes over Beirut once again, much to Reagan's displeasure. With civilian casualties increasing and television viewers watching plumes of smoke rising over Lebanon's capital, Reagan called Israeli Prime Minister Menachem Begin and asked him to stop the bombing.

"Menachem," he said, "this is a holocaust."

"Mr. President," the prime minister replied, "I think I know what a holocaust is." The Israelis called off their air assault.[1]

In an attempt to stabilize the region and allow diplomacy to work, Reagan agreed to deploy marines to Beirut International Airport as part of a multilateral peacekeeping force. They arrived in August 1982, and for a while, peace did indeed break out, so much so that the marines returned to ships offshore on September 10. But within a week, Lebanon was in flames again. The nation's newly elected president, Bashir Gemayel, was murdered. Israel moved troops into West Beirut despite promises that it would not do so. Syria allowed Iranian agents to operate on Lebanese soil near the Syrian border. Christian militia slaughtered hundreds of Palestinian civilians in refugee camps while Israeli forces nearby did nothing to intervene. The Soviets accused the Reagan administration of being party to a "bloody orgy."[2]

Lebanon was getting worse, not better. Reagan ordered the marines back, but any hope that they might be able to restore order was shattered on April 18, 1983, when a truck bomb exploded outside the U.S. Embassy in Beirut. Sixty-three people were killed, including several high-ranking CIA officials. That night, Reagan wrote in his diary: "Lord, forgive me for the hatred I feel for these humans who can do such a cruel but cowardly deed."[3]

Unlike conventional wars, there was no enemy to punish, no target to identify, nobody against whom the United States could lash out. A terrorist group with connections to Iran took credit for the attack, but even then, there was little Washington could do but fume, and mourn. Several days after the bombing, Reagan and the First Lady were at Andrews Air Force Base when the bodies of the victims were brought home. "I was too choked up to speak," he wrote.[4]

The administration pushed forward with diplomacy to little avail. Lebanon was a free-fire zone where Israelis, Syrians, Palestinians, Iranian revolutionaries, fundamentalist Muslims, and Christian militias contested each other in a deadly spectacle of bloodshed. Marines were caught in the middle, their peacekeeping mission literally under fire from militia who saw the Americans as enforcers for Lebanon's failing Christian minority government. In September 1983, the administration approved the use of Navy firepower to wipe out antigovernment militia positions. A mission designed to keep peace was transformed into something that seemed a good deal like war making.

Amid these challenges, Reagan's national security advisor, William Clark, resigned to take over the less demanding post of Interior Secretary; his deputy, McFarlane, replaced him. A round of furious White House intrigue followed as Reagan's badly divided advisors lobbied the president about the vacancy. Reagan decided to offer the coveted post to his chief of staff, James Baker, but then withdrew the offer because of opposition to Baker's proposed replacement as chief of staff, media guru Mike Deaver. With Baker out of the picture, Jeanne Kirkpatrick, Reagan's ambassador to the UN, lobbied for the job, but Reagan named McFarlane. On the morning of October 21, when he woke up the president with news from the Caribbean, McFarlane had been on the job just four days.

Several hours after learning of the disaster in Lebanon, Reagan flew back to Washington to monitor events on two fronts: the aftermath of the bombing, and the impending assault on Grenada. On Monday night, October 24, Reagan summoned congressional leaders for a briefing which the White House described as top secret. The politicians were instructed to tell nobody, including their spouses, that they were going to the White House.

The five congressional leaders assumed they were to be briefed about Lebanon. Instead, they were told about the operation about to get underway in Grenada. They were taken by surprise, and they were not alone. As the president and his aides explained the operation to the leaders, with Reagan emphasizing the potential danger to the American medical students on the island, a furious Margaret Thatcher called the White House. Reagan excused himself from the White House living quarters, where the briefing was taking place, to take the prime minister's call. She had heard of the impending invasion through intelligence sources. Grenada was a member of the British Commonwealth, and as such, was vaguely within Britain's sphere of influence. Thatcher demanded that her friend and ally call off the invasion, but it was too late.

Nineteen hundred U.S. soldiers landed on the island before dawn. Some seized control of an airport under construction—the Reagan administration had been insisting that the airstrip was designed for military purposes. Other troops fanned out to protect the American medical students. Cuban and Grenadan troops resisted, stiffly in places, but within twenty-four hours, the United States sent in Rangers, Navy SEALS, and members of the Army's elite Delta Force to suppress the island's defenders. Nineteen U.S. soldiers were killed and more than a hundred wounded. Forty-five Grenadan troops and twenty-four Cuban soldiers were killed, along with about two dozen civilians. The American medical students suffered no casualties.

The invasion was nearly flawless, and while Grenada was hardly Normandy or Okinawa, the operation won overwhelming support from the public. In a lightning strike, Reagan and the troops seemed to exorcize the ghosts of Vietnam and the failure and impotence of the Carter years.

On October 27, the president addressed the nation to discuss the disaster in Lebanon and the success in Grenada. It had been an exhausting few days, but Reagan betrayed none of the weariness he surely must have felt in his seventy-two-year-old bones as he explained what had happened in the Middle East and in the Caribbean.

He spoke first about the marines in Beirut, and sought, as House Speaker Tip O'Neill implored him to do during the briefing on Grenada, to explain why the marines were there in the first place, and why the United States could not afford to stand by while the Middle East descended into chaos. The "strategic importance" of the region, he said, was a key "to the economic and political life of the West ... If that key should fall into the hands of a power or powers hostile to the free world, there would be a direct threat to the United States and our allies." The Cold War context, then, justified the U.S. presence in Lebanon. The marines helped to give "the hard work of diplomacy" a chance at success. Despite the disaster, he said, the marines would remain in Beirut.

"To answer those who ask if we're serving any purpose in being there," he said, "let me answer a question with a question. Would the terrorists have launched their suicide attacks against the multinational force if it were not doing its job? The multinational force was attacked precisely because it is doing the job it was sent to do in Beirut. It is accomplishing its mission."

As he so often did, Reagan used anecdotes to illustrate or justify sweeping geopolitical strategies. "Let us meet our responsibilities," he said. "For longer than any of us can remember, the people in the Middle East have lived from war to war with no prospect for any other future. That dreadful cycle must be broken. Why are we there? Well, a Lebanese mother told one of our ambassadors that her little girl had only attended school two of the last eight years. Now, because of our presence there, she said her daughter could live a normal life."

With that homey anecdote, Reagan transitioned from the Middle East to the Caribbean. Grenada, he said, became a Marxist outpost with the rise of Maurice Bishop, "a protégé of Fidel Castro," as prime minister. But recently Bishop "gave indications that he might like better relations with the United States … Whether he was serious or not, we'll never know." He was ousted by the coup and then murdered, leading to the chain of events that ended with the U.S. invasion.

Reagan explained that the United States acted as it did because Grenada's neighbors asked it to intervene, and because a thousand U.S. civilians lived on the island. The specter of U.S. citizens being taken hostage was not far from the public's mind. "The nightmare of our hostages in Iran," he said, "must never be repeated."

Reagan spent far less time justifying Grenada than he did defending the U.S. presence in Lebanon. That was a reflection, of course, of victory and defeat. Victory requires no explanations. Failure and defeat do.

In summing up the success in the Caribbean, Reagan told a story told to him by General P.X. Kelley, commandant of the Marine Corps. Kelley told Reagan, and Reagan told the nation, of "a young marine" who was wounded during the assault on Grenada. "He couldn't see very well," Reagan quoted Kelley as saying. But when he realized he was in the presence of his commanding officer, he indicated that he wanted to write down a message. "We put a pad of paper in his hand," Reagan quoted from Kelley's account, "and he wrote, 'Semper Fi.'

"Well, if you've been a marine or if, like myself, you're an admirer of the marines, you know those words are a battle cry, a greeting, and a legend in the Marine Corps. They're marine shorthand for the motto of the Corps—'Semper Fidelis—always faithful.'"

Ronald Reagan understood the power of such personal anecdotes, and he understood, too, that such stories, and success, could change America's perception of its armed forces and its troops, both so badly battered during Vietnam. He closed with a moving appeal to his fellow citizens.

"I will not ask you to pray for the dead, because they're safe in God's loving arms and beyond need of our prayers," he said. "I would like to ask you all—wherever you may be in this blessed land—to pray for these wounded young men and to pray for the bereaved families of those who gave their lives for our freedom."

The pain and horror of the Lebanon bombing could not be pushed aside, and, in any case, that was not Reagan's intention. And for all of his defiant talk, Reagan did order the marines out of that war-torn, tragic country several months later, a retreat that a fledgling Islamic militant movement noticed, and remembered.

The successful operation in Grenada, however, did overshadow the defeat in Lebanon, at least in the short term. The military's competence and Reagan's rhetoric persuaded many Americans that the age of impotence was, at last, over.

Ronald Reagan gives a speech on the 40th Anniversary of D–Day at Pointe du Hoc, Normandy, France

CHAPTER 17

The Boys of Pointe du Hoc

*Speech Commemorating the
Fortieth Anniversary of D-Day*
June 6, 1984, Normandy, France

TRACK 17

BY THE MID-1980S, THE WORLD WAR II GENERATION WAS PREPARING FOR retirement and, perhaps not as overtly, for its inevitable encounter with the end of life's journey. Anniversaries of the war's milestones—the beginning of the war in Europe on September 1, the bombing of Pearl Harbor on December 7, the Allied invasion of Europe on June 6, the celebration of V-E Day on May 8 and V-J Day on August 14—were beginning to fade from the public's consciousness. Baby boomers, the oldest of whom were now middle-aged, had milestones of their own to commemorate.

In 1984, the oldest veterans of the war were, like Reagan, well into their seventies, and even the youngest were about or nearly sixty. The actuarial tables contained an undeniable truth: many of these aging veterans and their spouses would not be present when the nation paused, as it would, to commemorate the fiftieth anniversary of their achievements in the 1990s.

Some already had passed away, including Private First Class Peter Zanatta, who landed on a killing ground code-named Omaha Beach during the initial assault at six-thirty in the morning on June 6, 1944. Private Zanatta survived Omaha and the subsequent Allied assault through northern France and into Nazi Germany, and he swore to his daughter that one day he would return to Normandy and place flowers on the graves of his buddies who were buried in the massive American cemetery on the bluffs above Omaha Beach. But time ran out on Private Zanatta; he died of cancer before ever visiting the green fields where his buddies lay.

Among the several anniversaries connected to World War II, few retained its hold in the public's imagination like D-Day. Most Americans didn't know, nor did they care, that there were many D-Days during the war—D-Day is military parlance for the day on which an attack takes place. In popular memory, there was only one D-Day, and it was June 6, 1944, the day when the Allies landed on the beaches of northern France after sailing a hundred miles across the English Channel.

For Americans as well as Europeans, no other battle on the Western front symbolized the purity of the Allied cause more than D-Day. As Franklin Roosevelt phrased it during a nationwide radio address on the night of June 6, the Allied troops fought "not for the lust of conquest, but to end conquest."

And so, in 1984, the old Allied alliance decided to commemorate the fortieth anniversary of the invasion with the kind of pomp and circumstance usually associated with more numerically significant anniversaries. Heads of state and government from North America and Europe would convene on the hallowed ground of Normandy to commemorate and celebrate not just the remarkable feat of arms that took place on June 6, 1944, but all that the Allied cause represented in World War II—a mission to "set free a suffering humanity," as President Roosevelt put it on that June day forty years earlier.

Ronald Reagan was wearing a uniform on June 6, 1944, but he was not a combat soldier. He was assigned to the motion picture unit of the Army Air Corps, and was based in California. Nevertheless, he understood the mythic nature of D-Day and the place it held in the memory of those who lived through it, whether they were on the beaches or at home, waiting for news. Somebody else in the White House got it, too: presidential speech-writer Peggy Noonan. She was born six years after the invasion, but she, too, appreciated the bravery, the audacity, of that long day in 1944 when the fate of the Western Front was at stake. Noonan started working as one of several presidential speechwriters in April 1984, only two months before the D-Day anniversary. An unabashed fan of the president, she was astonished to learn that there were several layers of staff between her work and Reagan's desk. Powerful aides like James Baker could cut entire passages from speeches without the president ever having seen the original. But Noonan found a champion in Deputy Chief of Staff Richard Darman, who appreciated the literary touches in her speeches.

Noonan was assigned the task of writing a speech for Reagan's appearance at the ceremonies in Normandy. It would be timed to coincide with the live morning network shows back home, offering Reagan a priceless opportunity to speak to a national audience during a reelection campaign about some of his favorite topics—courage, patriotism, and sacrifice.

The president actually delivered two speeches during the long day of commemorations and tributes, but the first is rightly remembered as one of the finest he ever gave. He stood near the edge of steep cliffs on a spit of land called Pointe du Hoc. In the distance to Reagan's right, to the east, was the beach code-named Omaha, where American troops suffered the invasion's stiffest resistance. German gunners high above the beach may have been caught by surprise that morning—the weather had been so dreadful that few in the German high command believed the Allies would risk a landing in heavy seas and low visibility—but they recovered quickly. Wave after wave of U.S. soldiers were pinned down, unable to break through until late in the afternoon.

On June 6, 1944, more than two hundred Army Rangers scaled hundred-foot cliffs using ladders and grappling hooks while under murderous fire. Those who survived the climb faced lethal machine gun fire from a massive concrete pillbox a few hundred yards inland. The Rangers put it out of action, but couldn't destroy it—forty years later, it remained part of the landscape at Pointe du Hoc.

Sea winds whipped through Reagan's hair as he began the speech Peggy Noonan had prepared for him. It was a brilliant afternoon on the Normandy coast. Behind him, the Channel and the horizon were a brilliant blue. Lurking over Reagan's right shoulder was a high, craggy triangle of rock jutting into the Channel.

Gathered in front of the president were the men who survived the climb and the battles that followed. They were graying, their faces showing signs of age and wear. Reagan thought they looked like elderly businessmen. But forty years earlier, they were U.S. Army Rangers, young, strapping men given the seemingly suicidal assignment of scaling a cliff under fire during one of the most-storied military operations in history.

"We stand on a lonely, windswept point on the northern shore of France," Reagan said. "The air is soft, but forty years ago at this moment, the air was dense with smoke and the cries of men, and the air was filled with the crack of rifle fire and the roar of cannon." He recounted the impossible mission given to the Rangers, the fortitude they displayed, and the price they paid. "Two hundred and twenty-five came here," he noted. "After two days of fighting, only ninety could still bear arms …

"These are the boys of Pointe du Hoc," he said, gesturing to his audience seated in the field before him. "These are the men who took the cliffs. These are the champions who helped free a continent. These are the heroes who helped end a war."

Reagan's delivery and timing were never better. His words captured perfectly this moment of remembrance and tribute. The boys of Pointe du Hoc began to weep quietly, and they were not alone. Some in the hard-bitten press corps were teary as well as Reagan spoke not to the cameras, but to the men directly in front of him, the boys of Pointe du Hoc and other D-Day veterans from Allied countries.

"Forty summers have passed since the battle that you fought here. You were young the day you took these cliffs; some of you were hardly more than boys, with the deepest joys of life before you. Yet, you risked everything here. Why? Why did you do it? What impelled you to put aside the instinct for self-preservation and risk your lives to take these cliffs? What inspired all the men of the armies that met here? We look at you, and somehow we know the answer. It was faith and belief; it was loyalty and love.

"You all knew that some things are worth dying for. One's country is worth dying for, and democracy is worth dying for, because it's the most deeply honorable form of government ever devised by man. All of you loved liberty. All of you were willing to fight tyranny, and you knew the people of your countries were behind you."

With his ear for the small details that make a story, Reagan reminded his audience that while the Rangers scaled Pointe du Hoc, while the British, Canadians, Poles, Free French, and other allies established beach-heads along the coast, while Americans secured Utah Beach and improvised on Omaha, "word of the invasion was spreading through the darkness back home … in Georgia they were filling the churches at 4:00 a.m., in Kansas they were kneeling on porches and praying, and in Philadelphia they were ringing the Liberty Bell." The imagery of a pious nation gathered in prayer while brave men put their lives at risk was no mere rhetorical prop for Reagan, a devout man in his later years, one who would say without a trace of sophisticated irony that God was on the Allied side on that morning in France.

Significantly, Reagan mentioned an ally that was not present on D-Day because it was engaged in a titanic struggle of its own thousands of miles to the east. "It's fitting to remember here the great losses also suffered by the Russian people during World War II," he said. "Twenty million perished, a terrible price that testifies to all the world the necessity for ending war." In a beat, Reagan moved from tales of past bravery to the concerns of the moment. "I tell you from my heart that we in the United States do not want war. We want to wipe from the face of the Earth the terrible weapons that man now has in his hands. And I tell you, we are ready to seize that beachhead." He asked for a sign from America's former ally, the Soviet Union, that "they share our desire and love for peace, and that they will give up the ways of conquest."

He closed with an appeal to the world to "stand for the ideals" represented by the men in front of him. But he was not finished, not on this day of remembrance. After his stirring speech at Pointe du Hoc, Reagan drove to another ceremony, this one at Omaha Beach. There, to a new audience, he told the story of Private First Class Peter Zanatta, and his lifelong wish to visit the friends he lost in France in 1944. He read from a letter written by Zanatta's daughter, Lisa Zanatta Henn, who remembered hearing from her father stories of the courage it took to leap out of landing craft and into the firestorm of German resistance. His friends were killed before his eyes but, he explained to his daughter, "You did what you had to do, and you kept going."

Reagan told this international audience of one man's battle, one man's remembrance, and one man's vain dream of one day placing flowers on the graves of his friends, forever young. Before he died, in 1976, he heard his daughter make a promise: "I'm going there, Dad, and I'll put flowers there just like you wanted to do. I'll feel all the things you made me feel through your stories and your eyes. I'll never forget what you want through, Dad, nor will I let anyone else forget. And Dad, I'll always be proud."

Ronald Reagan's love of personal anecdotes taken from otherwise anonymous men and women was rarely better served that it was on June 6,

1984. He told his listeners that Peter Zanatta's daughter was in their midst, in Normandy on this day to make good on her last promise to her father.

"It is enough for us to say about Private Zannata and all the men of honor and courage who fought beside him four decades ago: We will always remember. We will always be proud. We will always be prepared, so we may always be free."

Ronald Reagan would go on to make many more speeches as president. Few were as memorable or as meaningful as those he delivered on June 6, 1984.

Ronald Reagan greets former U.S. Rangers at Pointe du Hoc

Ronald Reagan gives his acceptance speech at the 1984 Republican National Convention in Dallas, Texas

CHAPTER 18

A Stumble, and a Comeback

Debates between President Reagan and
Former Vice President Walter Mondale
October 7, 1984, and October 21, 1984

TRACK 18

A S A CANDIDATE TRYING TO UNSEAT INCUMBENT PRESIDENT JIMMY CARTER IN 1980, Ronald Reagan rose to the occasion when he and Carter faced each other in a nationally televised debate. His masterful performance was remembered for his off-handed dismissal of Carter's criticisms— "There you go again"—and his straightforward appeal to pocketbook issues. "Are you better off than you were four years ago?" he asked.

The debate helped turn the 1980 election into an electoral college landslide for Reagan. Four years later, as Reagan campaigned for reelection and prepared to debate his Democratic challenger, former Vice President Walter Mondale, few observers were inclined to underestimate his ability to perform in such a high-stakes event. After four years in the White House, he was a tested veteran of political give-and-take. He surely was known best for his heavily orchestrated set-piece speeches, but during his three-plus years as president, he submitted to more than two dozen nationally televised news conferences with the White House press corps, where questions were often unpredictable and always required the president to think on his feet. With that kind of experience, Reagan might well have relished the prospect of debating Jimmy Carter's vice president, who was vulnerable to a reprise of Reagan's successful criticisms of the Carter years.

Mondale was the favorite son of the Democratic Party establishment, but he had some trouble fending off surprisingly strong challenges from Colorado Senator Gary Hart, who portrayed Mondale as a symbol of the Democratic Party's recent failures, and from the Rev. Jesse Jackson.

By the summer of 1984, Ronald Reagan's political resurrection from the depths of early 1983 was nearly complete. The long and painful recession of 1981–82 was over, the disaster in Beirut had been overshadowed by success in Grenada, and U.S. involvement in the wars of Central America simply failed to register with a public accustomed to treating events south of the border as peripheral to the twilight struggle with the Soviets. Reagan's approval rating hit bottom in January 1983, when it was 35 percent, and began climbing when, not coincidentally, interest rates, unemployment figures, and inflation began to fall. What's more, his D-Day speeches, delivered not long before the two parties met for their presidential nominating conventions, positioned Reagan as a spokesman for America's image of itself as a selfless and courageous crusader for liberty. The president's reelection team captured, or perhaps created, the country's mood in a visually rich television commercial celebrating "morning in America." By late summer, Reagan's approval ratings approached 60 percent.

Mondale, then, faced an uphill battle as Democrats convened in San Francisco for their convention in July. He hoped to capitalize on some of the disparities in the country's economic recovery: more than thirteen million children lived in poverty, the largest number in decades, and family income among African Americans actually fell by 3.7 percent during Reagan's first term.[1] But Reagan's sunny message of a resurgent America caught on, despite the uneven numbers.

Mondale, known for his solid dependability rather than his dramatic flair, tried to capture the public's imagination with two bold gestures. First, he named Congresswoman Geraldine Ferraro of New York to be his running mate, making her the first woman nominated by a major party for national office. Then, in his acceptance speech, Mondale made one of the most astonishing promises in U.S. political history. "Let's tell the truth," Mondale said as he spoke of the task awaiting the winner of the '84 election. "Mr. Reagan will raise taxes, and so will I. He won't tell you. I just did."

The delegates in San Francisco's Moscone Center burst into applause, delighted with their candidate's uncharacteristic boldness and his willingness to confront unpleasant truths. As Reagan's supporters watched the speech on television, they, too, cheered. Mondale, they believed, had sealed his fate. Americans who chose Ronald Reagan's antigovernment, antitax message in 1980 were not about to reverse course in favor of an avowed tax-raiser.

As the Democrats dispersed from California, the athletes of the world— except those from the Soviet bloc—poured into the state for the 1984 Summer Olympics in Los Angeles. The Soviets and their allies boycotted the games in retaliation for the U.S.-led boycott of the 1980 games in Moscow, called to protest the Russian invasion of Afghanistan. Without the Russians and the Eastern Europeans, the United States won gold medals by the dozens. Reagan was on hand for the proceedings and was interviewed on national television, basking in the glow of American achievement.

As the two candidates prepared for the first of two scheduled debates in early October, Reagan held a commanding lead in the polls. Mondale and the Democrats attacked Reagan for favoring the rich over the poor in his economic policy, and for favoring fantasy over reality in pushing his Star Wars initiative. Neither criticism caught on, but Reagan's aides were concerned about a Democratic attack on the president's competence and command. In the days before the debate, Reagan sat through several intense briefings on social and economic policy, the twin themes of the debate. Budget director David Stockman played the role of Mondale in several mock sessions with Reagan. The young aide was so relentless and aggressive with his boss that when the rehearsals were finished, Reagan told Stockman, "You'd better send me some flowers, because you've been nasty to me."[2] The president might have been joshing, but his confidence was shaken.

Reagan and Mondale met in the Kentucky Center for the Arts in Louisville on October 7. They faced questions from James Wieghart of the Scripps-Howard News Service, Fred Barnes of the *Baltimore Sun*, and Diane Sawyer of CBS News. Barbara Walters served as the evening's moderator. Reagan took his place at a podium to the right of the panel, while Mondale was on the left.

The evening's focus on domestic issues figured to play to Reagan's strengths. The economy was Reagan's top priority from Day One, and now, in the last few weeks of his reelection campaign, he could—and did—take credit for helping to produce an economic recovery.

But Mondale defied expectations with an aggressive and at times humorous attack on the president's policies. After hearing the president defend his stewardship of Social Security, Mondale replied, "I'm reminded a little bit of what Will Rogers once said about [Herbert] Hoover. He said, 'It's not what he doesn't know that bothers me; it's what he knows for sure that just ain't so.'" Mondale, never known for his impish wit, quickly stole the stage from his anecdote-loving opponent, who struggled to recall the facts and figures in his briefing book. After Mondale suggested that Reagan would have no choice but to raise taxes if he were reelected, the president reached back for a line from his debate with Mondale's former boss, Jimmy Carter. "You know," Reagan said, "I wasn't going to say this at all, but I can't help it. There you go again." He denied that he had a plan to increase taxes, but Mondale could barely contain himself until it was his turn to reply. His body language and facial expression showed that he had been waiting for Reagan to bring out his laugh line from four years ago.

Breaking from the format, he addressed Reagan directly. "Mr. President, you said, 'There you go again,' right?"

"Yes," Reagan said, not sensing he was about to fall into a trap.

"You remember the last time you said that?" Mondale asked with all the assurance of a prosecutor grilling an obviously guilty defendant. Reagan, now wary, acknowledged that he remembered saying the line before.

"You said it when President Carter said that you were going to cut Medicare, and you said, 'Oh, no, there you go again, Mr. President.'" Mondale said. "And what did you do right after the election? You went out and tried to cut $20 billion out of Medicare. And so, when you say, 'There you go again'—people remember this, you know." Reagan was floored. He tried to regroup. "I never proposed any $20 billion should come out of Medicare; I have proposed that the program ... we must treat with that particular problem," he said, stumbling. He tried to reach into the figures in those briefing books, but could only flail about.

As the debate drew to a close, moderator Barbara Walters invited the candidates, beginning with Reagan, to give their set-piece closing remarks. But after she cued Reagan, she interrupted to note that the president had not been given a chance to make one final rebuttal. Unsure of what to do, her director giving her cues in her earpiece, Walters tried to let Reagan know that he didn't have to give his closing statement just yet, if he wished to respond to Mondale one last time.

"I'm all confused now," Reagan said. He looked and sounded older than he had even an hour earlier. His face seemed to sag; his voice lost its command. He was no longer president of the United States, but an elderly neighbor who had forgotten where he lived.

Years later, Reagan admitted that he "nearly blew the whole race during my first debate with Mondale."[3] The person closest to the president, his wife Nancy, was furious. "What have you done to my husband," she angrily asked aide Michael Deaver.[4]

The president's performance raised the question of his age. While Reagan clearly looked younger than his seventy-three years and was in superb physical health, suddenly his memory and command were in question. The wave of speculation about Reagan's competence—precisely the issue his supporters feared that Mondale would have seized upon weeks earlier—as well as the public discussion of his age, worried the president and his team. Reagan was unhappy with his performance in Louisville—"I take pride in my public speaking ability," he wrote. An election that seemed a foregone conclusion was on the verge of becoming a much tighter race.

The two men met again on October 21 in the Municipal Auditorium in Kansas City, Missouri. The ostensible topic was foreign relations, but, in fact, Ronald Reagan's competency was the unspoken theme of the evening. Once again, Mondale was animated and aggressive, zeroing in on a revelation that the Contras in Nicaragua were using a CIA-supplied assassination manual that advocated the murder of Sandinista government officials. Reagan's replies and his own attacks were far more coherent and organized than they had been in Louisville. He got a laugh when he noted that one of Mondale's campaign commercials showed the candidate on the flight deck of the aircraft carrier U.S.S. *Nimitz*, watching F-14's take off. The president noted that Mondale had been against construction of the *Nimitz*.

Finally, though, one of the reporters on the panel, the *Baltimore Sun's* Henry Trewhitt, addressed what for many Americans was the debate's main issue: Ronald Reagan's mental fitness for another term. "You already are the oldest president in history," Trewhitt said. "And some on your staff say you were tired after your most recent encounter with Mr. Mondale. I recall … that President Kennedy had to go days on end with very little sleep during the Cuban missile crisis. Is there any doubt in your mind that you would be able to function in such circumstances?"

Reagan would later say that he did not anticipate such a question, which was, by polite standards of presidential debate decorum, very personal and almost painful to watch. But Reagan did not flinch. "Not at all, Mr. Trewhitt," he said, making sure to mention the reporter by name and to answer his question. He had no doubts that he could function "in such circumstances."

Then, Reagan added: "And I want you to know that also I will not make age an issue in this campaign. I am not going to exploit, for political purposes, my opponent's youth and inexperience." The audience, and Mondale, burst into laughter.

By most accounts, Reagan's supporters breathed a long sigh of relief. Though the president came in for tough grilling from Mondale, Reagan's line about his opponent's "youth and inexperience" grabbed the next day's headlines.

A week later, on Tuesday, November 5, Ronald Wilson Reagan won a reelection victory of historic proportions. He took forty-nine states—all but Mondale's home state of Minnesota and the District of Columbia. Fifty-three million Americans voted for him, compared with thirty-six million for Mondale. The significance of the victory went beyond numbers. It spoke of a reordering of late 20th century American politics. As one of Mondale's supporters, future Labor Secretary Robert Reich, put it: "Reagan has presided over a triumph of ideas."[5]

PART THREE

The Second Term

1985–89

Ronald Reagan and Mikhail Gorbachev at the first summit in Geneva, Switzerland

Introduction

T
AX REFORM, SCANDAL, AND AN ASTONISHING BREAKTHROUGH IN THE COLD
War marked Ronald Reagan's second term. Historically, if first
terms produce dramatic change, second terms institutionalize
those changes. That seemed to be the case with Reagan, until he and Soviet
leader Mikhail Gorbachev formed a partnership that led to the end of the
twilight struggle between the United States and the Soviet Union in the
final months of Reagan's presidency.

Tax reform was among Reagan's top priorities as his second term
opened, eventually leading to a tax simplification law that reduced the
number of tax brackets from fourteen to three. Reagan considered tax
reform the last important piece of his program to reduce the burden on
American taxpayers.

Reagan's attempts to destabilize the Nicaraguan government were a
good deal less popular than his tax reductions, leading Democrats in
Congress to bar U.S. military aid to a group of rebels, the Contras,
attempting to overthrow the Sandinistas. At the same time, Reagan was
increasingly concerned about American citizens who were falling prey to
hostage-takers in the Middle East. Administration officials secretly
reached out to the Iranian government, a pariah since the hostage crisis of
1979, in hopes that Iran would use its influence to free the hostages. In
return, the United States promised to sell Iran weapons covertly, through

Israeli intermediaries. The proceeds of those covert sales were to be funneled, illegally, to the Contras.

The Iran-Contra deal became public in late 1986. The public and Congress were outraged. Reagan denied that he had traded arms for hostages, but soon afterwards he admitted that his administration had done exactly that. Congressional hearings and an independent investigation would bring to light clandestine operations run out of the White House with the knowledge and approval of top Reagan administration officials. The question was how much the president himself knew about the affair. A commission chaired by former Texas Senator John Tower concluded that Reagan was out of touch with the operations of his own administration.

Reagan seemed no more than a shadow president for much of 1987, a hostage to the Iran-Contra scandal. But as the clock wound down on his administration, historic changes were underway behind the Iron Curtain. Mikhail Gorbachev's reform program signaled the end of the old Soviet Union, and Reagan eagerly grasped the opportunity to change East-West relations. As time began to run out on the Reagan years, the United States and Soviet Union signed an historic treaty drastically reducing their nuclear forces in Europe. Reagan and Gorbachev took turns visiting their respective countries.

Forty years of tensions between the United States and the U.S.S.R. were coming to an end, under the tenure of a man who so recently described the Soviet Union as an evil empire.

Reagan's popularity rebounded, giving his vice president, George H.W. Bush, the bounced he needed. Running as heir to the Reagan Revolution, Bush handily defeated Democrat Michael Dukakis in the 1988 election.

Ronald Reagan left Washington on January 21, 1989. The world had changed during his eight years as president thanks in part to his words, his ideas, and his role as one of the great political communicators of the 20th century.

The Reagans greet freshman Senator John McCain during a dinner for newly elected members of the 100th Congress in 1987

Reagan is sworn in at the White House for his second term as President

CHAPTER 19

A World Lit by Lightning

Ronald Reagan's
Second Inaugural Address
January 21, 1985

TRACK 19

WASHINGTON DC IS RARELY AS COLD AS IT WAS ON MONDAY MORNING, January 21, 1985, when 73-year-old Ronald Reagan became the oldest person to take the oath of office as president, breaking the record he set in 1981, when he became president just shy of his seventieth birthday. Temperatures in Washington hovered around ten degrees, forcing the cancellation of the outdoor pomp and ceremony that traditionally follows the president's inaugural address. Reagan took the oath and delivered his inaugural address in the Capitol Rotunda rather than on the building's west portico.

When Reagan raised his right hand to take the oath from Chief Justice Warren Burger on January 21, he already was a day into his second term. The Constitution mandates that presidential terms expire and new ones begin at noon on January 20. But custom dictates that when the date falls on a Sunday, as was the case in 1985, the public swearing-in, the inaugural address, and the parades and balls are held the following day. Reagan took the oath in a quick, private ceremony in the White House on January 20, and then repeated the process in front of television cameras and hundreds of assembled guests huddled together in the Rotunda the following afternoon.

Ronald Reagan was not the first president of the 20th century to be reelected with a gigantic mandate. His former hero, Franklin Roosevelt, mauled Alf Landon in 1936, Dwight Eisenhower easily won his rematch with Adlai Stevenson in 1956, and Richard Nixon overwhelmed George McGovern in 1972. But only Roosevelt's reelection in '36 was as historically significant as Reagan's in 1984. FDR's victory solidified a coalition that would go on to dominate U.S. politics for more than two decades. Reagan's reelection institutionalized the changes in policy, rhetoric, and emphasis that the president implemented during his first term. Slightly more than a decade after Reagan's reelection, a popular Democratic president, Bill Clinton, would announce that "the era of big government is over." By the mid-1990s, even Democrats often sounded like Reaganites.

The new term meant continuity at the top but changes elsewhere in the Reagan White House. In early January, Treasury Secretary Donald Regan and Chief of Staff James Baker approached the president about trading jobs. Reagan readily agreed, much to Regan's shock—the new chief of staff didn't realize that the president knew in advance of the Baker-Regan deal because his wife Nancy had been tipped off by Deputy Chief of Staff Michael Deaver. Regan, a tough-talking police officer's son from South Boston who went on to become chairman of Merrill Lynch, quickly streamlined the White House chain of command to give his office more power over access to the president. Baker, politically ambitious and eager for a higher profile, hoped the new Cabinet post would lead to a presidential campaign one day. Six months into the new term, Deaver himself left the White House for the private sector.

In the days leading up to Inauguration Day, Reagan set out his priorities for the new term. He told Regan that he wanted to cut federal spending, reduce a deficit that had spiraled out of control during his first four years, simplify the nation's famously complicated tax code, and produce an arms reduction treaty with the Soviets. Central America remained an important priority—Reagan was no less committed to the Contras than he was before the election. And the Middle East figured to loom larger than it had during Reagan's first term, when the region was peripheral to the president's agenda for Europe and Central America. The Islamic terrorist group Hezbollah held six Americans hostage as the president prepared for his new term. One of those hostages was the CIA's station chief in Beirut, William

Buckley, who would later be tortured and murdered. Reagan, who owed his victory in 1980 in part to American anger over the Iranian hostage crisis, now understood how Jimmy Carter felt in 1979. "No problem was more frustrating for me when I was president than trying to get the American hostages home," he wrote. "It was a problem I shared with Jimmy Carter."[1]

As with any second-term president, particularly one with a strong mandate, there was much talk of the president's place in history as he embarked on his second term. Most of the discussion centered on his domestic record—his tax cuts, his reductions in social spending, and increases in military spending, and, irony of ironies, his apparent embrace of deficit financing. As he began his new term, Ronald Reagan, fiscal conservative, was staring at deficit projections of some $200 billion a year, an unprecedented figure.

Reagan's record on the international stage was less remarked upon, no doubt because there was not very much to say. There had been no diplomatic triumphs during the president's first term, nothing akin to Jimmy Carter's mediation between Israel and Egypt, or Richard Nixon's stunning trip to Communist China. Reagan certainly was more confrontational in his Cold War rhetoric, but those words had led to nothing more than sparring matches and a general chilliness between the superpowers. Conflicts in Central America, the Middle East, and Central Asia remained unresolved, fueled in part by U.S. support for anti-Communist guerillas in Afghanistan, rebels in Nicaragua, and government forces in El Salvador.

So, as the president prepared for another four years, journalists and historians were watching eagerly for clues to see how Ronald Reagan would use one of the greatest mandates ever given an incumbent president. Would the second term see breakthroughs around the globe, or would it simply seek to consolidate the Reagan Revolution at home?

Washington's elite donned heavy topcoats, scarves and gloves for the journey to the Capitol on the morning of January 21 for Ronald Reagan's second inaugural address. Cabinet members, Supreme Court justices, and members of Congress hurried into the warmth of the Capitol Rotunda. The ornate room, decorated with statues of American political icons, had been hastily converted into a reception hall, with rows of folding chairs placed in front of and behind a lectern decorated with the presidential seal. It was close and perhaps a bit uncomfortable, but at least it was warm.

Reagan was dressed in a blue suit, striped tie, and matching handkerchief in his left breast pocket. He began with the sort of personal touch that endeared him even to political foes like Speaker O'Neill. Reagan noted the presence in the room of Senator John Stennis, a Democrat from Mississippi, who had just returned to work after cancer surgery that required the amputation of his left leg. He then asked for a moment of prayer in memory of Representative Gillis Long, a Louisiana Democrat who died the previous evening.

Always eager to make historical connections in his speeches, Reagan noted that the ceremony was the fiftieth formal presidential inauguration—not counting the swearing-in of vice presidents to replace presidents who died or resigned. It was, he said, an occasion to look back, and to look ahead. "We have lighted the world with our inventions, gone to the aid of mankind wherever in the world there was a cry for help, journeyed to the moon and safely returned," he said. "So much has changed. And yet we stand together as we did two centuries ago."

Americans looking for clues about the president's second-term priorities had reason to conclude that Reagan II would offer more of the same intense focus on the economy and other domestic issues. In contrast to so many other Cold War inaugural addresses—except his own in 1981—Reagan pointedly stayed close to home in his themes and promises.

After reciting the domestic accomplishments of his first term—tax reduction, reduced inflation, higher employment—he reminded Americans of what they, too, had achieved, and how they would be remembered.

"These will be years when Americans have restored their confidence and tradition of progress; when our values of faith, family, work, and neighborhood were restated for a modern age; when our economy was finally freed from government's grip; when we made sincere efforts at meaningful arm reduction …

"My fellow citizens, our nation is poised for greatness. We must do what we know is right and do it with all our might. Let history say of us, 'These were golden years—when the American Revolution was reborn, when freedom gained new life, and America reached for her best.'"

That reborn revolution, he said, would "increase the rewards for work, savings, and investment; reduce the increase in the cost and size of government and its interference in people's lives."

After spending most of his speech on domestic issues, he turned to the Cold War, and to his vision of a world freed from the fear of nuclear destruction. The United States and the Soviet Union, he noted, "have lived under the threat of mutual assured destruction … Is there either logic or morality in believing that if one side threatens to kill tens of millions of our people, our only recourse is to threaten killing tens of millions of theirs?" Reagan reiterated his commitment to a missile defense system that, he said, "would render nuclear weapons obsolete."

Dismissed as a fantasy at best, a plot to enrich defense contractors at worst, Reagan's vision of a world free of nuclear weapons was authentic and earnest. But many still regarded it as an expensive fantasy.

As he neared the speech's conclusion, listeners could hear the timber of Reagan's voice beginning to reach for a crescendo with a torrent of words and images that spoke to his innermost beliefs in America and its exceptional nature.

"My friends," he said, "we live in a world that is lit by lightning. So much is changing and will change, but so much endures, and transcends time. History is a ribbon, always unfurling; history is a journey. As we continue our journey, we think of those who traveled before us." As he read the next line of his prepared text, he immediately realized it was out of date thanks to the weather, and he ad-libbed. "We stand again at the steps of this symbol of our democracy—or we would have been standing at the steps if it hadn't gotten so cold. Now we are standing inside this symbol of our democracy." The audience smiled in appreciation of the president's quick editing—this was not, after all, the Ronald Reagan they saw in the first debate with Walter Mondale. He finished with a flourish:

"And we see and hear again the echoes of our past: a general falls to his knees in the hard snow of Valley Forge; a lonely president paces the darkened halls, and ponders his struggle to preserve the Union; the men of the Alamo call out encouragement to each other; a settler pushes west and sings a song, and the song echoes out forever and fills the unknowing air.

"It is the American sound. It is hopeful, big-hearted, idealistic, daring, decent, and fair. That's our heritage; that is our song. We sing it still."

And few sang it louder than Ronald Reagan.

Ronald Reagan walks with General Matthew Ridgeway at Bitburg Cemetery

CHAPTER 20

A Painful Walk into the Past

Remarks at Bergen–Belsen Concentration Camp,
West Germany
May 5, 1985

TRACK 20

R ONALD REAGAN BELIEVED HE OWED WEST GERMAN CHANCELLOR HELMUT Kohl. Despite enormous political pressure, Kohl supported Reagan's plan to deploy U.S. intermediate-range missiles on German soil. His support for the American plan was critical, and politically risky. Reagan appreciated the German's refusal to back down in the face of the nuclear-freeze movement and other critics.

So when Kohl asked Reagan to join him for ceremonies in West Germany to mark the 40th anniversary of the end of World War II, the president readily agreed. Reagan was scheduled to be in West Germany anyway for a world economic summit in Bonn, the West German capital, in late April and early May 1985. After the summit, the two leaders would commemorate the anniversary together in a gesture of reconciliation and redemption.

The visit figured to be a reprise of the president's emotional and highly successful appearance in Normandy for the 40th anniversary of D-Day. The president and his speechwriters understood the narrative of World War II and its ongoing appeal to Americans, even those born well after the war's end. The war was a 20th century morality tale pitting good against evil, a necessary war that led to the redemptive triumph of freedom thanks to the selfless sacrifice of millions of soldiers and civilians. Reagan's appearance in

Germany for the anniversary offered the president another opportunity to frame the war in such heroic terms.

The White House issued the president's itinerary in early April. The list of joint appearances with Kohl included a visit to a German military cemetery in the town of Bitburg, home to a U.S. air base. The White House, known by now for its sensitive political antennae, was caught by surprise when Jewish groups and other Americans raised an outcry against the proposed visit. Some of the German troops buried in Bitburg fought against the United States in the Battle of the Bulge, one of war's bitterest battles on the Western Front. Reagan took note of the protests in his diary, but he expressed no doubts about the course he would take. "There is no way I'll back down and run for cover," he wrote. "What is wrong with saying, 'Let's never be enemies again?'"[1]

The original outcry was nothing compared with the protests that arose when the press revealed that nearly fifty SS officers were buried in Bitburg. The SS troops were not regular, rank-and-file German soldiers caught up in a war over which they had little control. The SS men were specially trained for murder. They staffed the concentration camps. They were Adolf Hitler's henchmen.

Reagan came under fire not only from his fellow Republicans but, privately, from his wife, Nancy, who opposed the visit on moral grounds and who feared for her husband's safety if he went through with the visit. To mollify the critics, the White House quickly added a visit to the Bergen-Belsen concentration camp to the president's schedule. Before the storm broke, Reagan had turned down a chance to visit the notorious Dachau camp.

On April 19, as criticism reached a fever pitch, Reagan took a phone call from Kohl. The German said that any cancellation of the Bitburg visit would be perceived as an insult to the German people. Reagan did not need to be reminded of the debt he felt he owed his ally. He assured Kohl that he had no intention of canceling.

Later that evening, by an astonishing coincidence, Reagan welcomed Holocaust survivor Elie Wiesel to the White House to receive the Congressional Gold Medal, the nation's highest civilian award. Wiesel survived Auschwitz and Buchenwald; his parents and a sister did not. After the war, he became a writer and a speaker who reminded the world of the abomination that the Jews of Europe had suffered. He was known around the world for his moral clarity and his courage—within a year, he would be named winner of the Nobel Peace Prize for his passionate advocacy of human rights and dignity, the very things that were denied him and millions of his fellow Jews during World War II.

In the Roosevelt Room of the White House, with the president sitting directly in front of him, Wiesel delivered a speech in acceptance of the award, which he said belonged not only to him but to "all those who remember what SS killers have done to their victims." While he praised his host for his efforts on behalf of Soviet Jews, Wiesel could not avoid Bitburg. His accented English filled the room with power and with almost unbearable tension.

"That place, Mr. President, is not your place," he said. "Your place is with the victims of the SS." He put the issue in terms Reagan surely would have recognized. "The issue here is not politics but good and evil," he said. "And we must never confuse them, for I have seen the SS at work, and I have seen their victims. They were my friends. They were my parents."[2]

Reagan may have been moved by the power of Wiesel's words, but he did not back down. Nor did his critics. A week later, the Senate passed a nonbinding resolution asking the West German government to withdraw its invitation to Reagan, which would offer the president an out without offending his ally. Reagan wrote in his diary: "Well, I don't want out. I think I am doing what is morally right."[3]

He flew to Bonn on April 29 and joined his fellow world leaders for talks on trade and other economic issues. Then, on May 5, after the summit broke up, he and Kohl and their wives proceeded as scheduled. They flew to Bergen-Belsen by helicopter, and walked through the preserved remains of the camp. They passed mounds covered in heather, marking the mass graves where some of the camp's sixty thousand dead were buried. Reagan kept his arm around his wife's waist as they toured a museum displaying horrifying images of the camp after the British liberated it in April 1945. Bodies stacked upon bodies; the bodies of men, women, and children.

They had not been gassed. Bergen-Belsen had none of the Nazi machinery of mass death. There were no gas chambers, no crematoria. But disease, overwork, and starvation were lethal enough.

Most of the victims met their death toward the end of the war, when the Nazis began shipping thousands of Jews to what had been designed as a detention camp for about ten thousand people. Some of Bergen-Belsen's prisoners were taken there from Auschwitz and other camps to the east, where the Germans were in retreat in the face of a massive Red Army assault. Among those who died at Bergen-Belsen in the war's final weeks was a fifteen-year-old Jewish girl from Amsterdam named Anne Frank.

After walking through the camp, Reagan, wearing a tan trench coat, his head bowed, carried a wreath to a memorial wall dedicated to the camp's victims. He then moved to a solitary lectern, very much alone. There were no smiling aides in the background or on either side of him. He looked shocked, for the power of the place was undiminished forty years after its liberation. Nancy Reagan, seated nearby, dabbed at her eyes.

He told his audience that he had just made a "painful walk into the past," where he was reminded of the "awful evil started by one man" and which led to "the grim abyss of these camps."

Reagan then cited the essential truth of the Holocaust: the human beings whose remains were buried nearby, the human beings who perished in other camps, died because they were Jews. They were not political opponents of the regime, not that such activity would justify their murders. They were not chosen for death arbitrarily. They were the victims of organized murder.

"Here lie people—Jews—whose death was inflicted for no reason other than their very existence," Reagan said. "Their pain was borne only because of who they were and because of the God in their prayers ... People were brought here for no other purpose but to suffer and die—to go unfed when hungry, uncared for when sick, tortured when the whim struck, and left to have misery consume them ..."

But even in this place that bore witness to humankind's capacity for evil, Reagan searched for redemption. That was utterly characteristic of the man. Biographer Lou Cannon noted of this visit that Reagan seemed uncomfortable when he faced the reality of genocide. He preferred the triumphant notes of history, not its often terrible tragedies and crimes. Confronted with inhumanity, he tried to find the solace of redemption.

"Here, death ruled," he said, "but we've learned something as well. Because of what happened, we found that death cannot rule forever, and that's why we're here today ... We're here to commemorate that life triumphed over the tragedy and the death of the Holocaust ... We're here today to confirm that the horror cannot outlast the hope, and that even from the worst of all things, the best may come forth." He quoted from the Talmud, which asserted that by their suffering "the children of Israel obtained three priceless and coveted gifts: The Torah, the Land of Israel, and the World to Come."

He closed with a quotation from the camp's most famous victim, Anne Frank, who died of typhus in March 1945, just weeks before the British liberated the camp. The girl's diary, found and published after the war, spoke of hope in the face of horror, and idealism in the face of inhumanity.

"I can feel the suffering of millions and yet, if I looked up into the heavens I think that it will all come out right, that this cruelty too will end and that peace and tranquility will return again," she wrote.

That spirit, Reagan suggested, did not die with Anne Frank.

"We're all witnesses," he said. "We share the glistening hope that rests in every human soul. Hope leads us, if we're prepared to trust it, toward what our President Lincoln called the better angels of our nature.

"And then, rising above all this cruelty, out of this tragic and nightmarish time, beyond the anguish, the pain, and the suffering for all time, we can and must pledge: Never again."

Reagan then left Bergen-Belsen for Bitburg. He was in the cemetery for fewer than ten minutes, and made no formal remarks. He hoped his words at Bergen-Belsen were sufficient. They were for some, but not for everybody. The criticism of Bitburg did not go away.

Ronald Reagan holds an oversized replica of a 1984 income tax form that has a black circle with a line across it

CHAPTER 21

A Second American Revolution

Address to the Nation on Tax Reform
May 28, 1985

TRACK 21

R ONALD REAGAN'S LANDSLIDE REELECTION IS UNIMAGINABLE WITHOUT THE economic recovery that began halfway into his term. While Reagan's sunny reelection theme—"It's morning again in America"—clearly referred to the successful invasion of Grenada and the perception that American foreign policy was in competent hands again, ultimately the slogan drew its power from a revived economy. Walter Mondale and his fellow Democrats tried to argue that the dawn of Reaganomics shone brightest for the rich, that workers displaced by the long recession of 1981–82 still struggled in darkness. But on Election Day, voters chose daybreak and optimism.

Reagan had been advocating for tax reduction since his days as a spokesman for General Electric, and given the chance to make good on his words, he implemented a 25-percent cut early on in his first term.

He never tired of pointing out that during his later Hollywood years, he was in the 94-percent tax bracket, and he saw how high taxes left many other actors with a mere fraction of their high salaries. But sweeping reductions were only part of his campaign against internal revenue policy. He wanted to make the system simpler, too.

Reagan spoke about tax simplification during his first term, most prominently during his State of the Union message in 1984, just as his reelection campaign was beginning. He told members of Congress that he would ask Treasury Secretary Donald Regan to devise a "plan of action to simplify the entire tax code so that all taxpayers, big and small, are treated more fairly." Tax simplification was, well, hardly a simple matter, and generally not the sort of issue politicians would take on during an election year. For that reason, as Reagan biographer Lou Cannon noted, after the president made his bold call to action on nothing less that the nation's revenue code, he added that Regan, the treasury secretary, would report back with his simplification proposal in December—after the '84 elections. According to Cannon, White House Chief of Staff James Baker made sure that simplification was placed on the back burner during the campaign season, regardless of how eager the president was to pursue it.[1]

The timetable was an obvious ploy, and Democrats knew it. As Cannon recalled, the House chamber "erupted in a gale of cynical laughter in an unusual sign of disrespect for the president."[2] State of the Union messages, or, for that matter, all presidential appearances on Capitol Hill, rarely inspire overt signs of partisan division. Democrats might sit on their hands when a Republican president proposes policies with which they disagree, and vice versa, but public displays of disagreement, not to mention cynicism, are avoided in the interest of decorum.

But Democrats were a frustrated bunch as the campaign season opened, and they were not opposed to showing it. Their derisive laughter was audible to the millions watching Reagan's speech on television, and to the president himself. He tried to continue reading his speech, but finally stopped and asked, "I said something funny?" He was genuinely perplexed, an innocent, in some ways, in a crowd of career politicians who had heard it all before. Reagan's proposal may have sounded bold and revolutionary to the audience at home, but to Washington veterans, the timetable mocked the president's call for change. The fine-sounding sentiments came with no real plan for implementation.

Or so it seemed. As Washington focused on Campaign '84, Regan and his team went to work on the tax code. They produced a plan slightly ahead of schedule, in mid-November. More remarkably, no details about the plan found their way into the press, an achievement in which Regan, who despised leaks, took particular pride.

The report proposed reducing the number of tax brackets in the revenue code from fourteen to just three. Earners in the top bracket would be taxed at a rate of 35 percent; those in the middle, 25 percent, and those at the bottom, 15 percent. Under existing tax law, the federal tax rate topped out at 50 percent, so the Regan proposal called for a significant reduction in the rate for the nation's wealthiest earners.

The plan also contained several other important changes. Taxpayers would no longer be allowed to deduct their state and local taxes on their federal tax form, a body blow aimed at states with high income taxes. Americans would be encouraged to save more for their old age through the creation of individual retirement accounts. Individual deductions would more than double, to $2,000, and top corporate tax rates would fall from nearly 50 percent to 33 percent.

The Regan plan was a significant initiative, and Reagan eagerly embraced it. On May 28, 1985, shortly after his return from Europe, the president addressed the nation on television to make his pitch for not just another tax bill, but a significant adjustment in the nation's tax policy.

Reagan, with his flair for drama and his love of history, called the plan nothing less than "a second American revolution." This one, he promised, would be "peaceful," but it was born of the same complaints that inspired the rebellion against King George III—"popular resentment against a tax system that is unwise, unwanted, and unfair."

Reagan was a familiar visitor to the living rooms of America by May 1985, and his tone and delivery reflected that perceived intimacy between the president and the public. His introduction was spare, plain, and to the point. "I'd like to speak to you tonight," he said, "about our future, about a great historic effort to give the words 'freedom,' 'fairness,' and 'hope' new meaning and power for every man and woman in America."

His choice of words was no accident, for he knew that Democrats, particularly his favorite sparring partner, Tip O'Neill, often criticized his domestic policies as unfair to the poor and middle class, as a source of hope only to the well-off. "Tip O'Neill used every opportunity he got to lambaste me as a 'rich man's president' who cared nothing about the little man, the unemployed, or the poor, and said my economic program was a 'cruel hoax,'" Reagan wrote about an earlier budget battle.[3] The terms of the debate hadn't changed since Reagan's first term, but now, the president hoped to reframe domestic policy with a plan that he believed would help all Americans.

"I've spoken with and received letters from thousands of you—Republicans, Democrats, and Independents," he said. "I know how hungry you are for change. Make no mistake, we—the sons and daughters of those first brave souls who came to this land to give birth to a new life in liberty—we can change America. We can change America forever. So, let's get started. Let's change the tax code to make it fairer and change tax rates so they're lower." Domestic policy, particularly tax bills, rarely were cast in such historic terms. But Reagan wished to persuade the nation that tinkering with the tax code wouldn't do. The time was ripe for sweeping change.

He knew that there were many enemies of change, and not all of them were Democratic members of the House of Representatives. Taxpayers themselves could be afraid of change, and for good reason. They knew what to expect from the old system; a new system might cost them money.

Anticipating that reaction, Reagan spoke directly to his listeners:

"I'll start by answering one question on your minds," he said. "Will our proposal help you? You bet it will. We call it America's tax plan because it will reduce tax burdens on the working people of this country, close loopholes that benefit a privileged few, simplify a code so complex even Albert Einstein reportedly needed help on his 1040 form, and lead us into a future of greater growth and opportunity for all."

It was a classic Reagan pitch: he cast himself as the true populist and enemy of privilege, he threw in a humorous but unverifiable anecdote to support his case (would anybody really care if it turned out that Einstein didn't require help on his tax form?), and pitched his plan as an advance for the cause of freedom and economic growth—concepts that were inextricably tied together in his mind.

As he often did, Reagan used anecdotes and letters to explain how his policy would work on behalf of ordinary Americans and at the expense of privileged elites—a rhetoric device few Republicans before him would have dared to try. But Reagan had spent years arguing that the status quo was a friend of the few and the enemy of the many, so he was completely comfortably playing the role of economic populist. "For three decades," he said, "families have paid the freight for the special interests. Now families are in trouble. As one man from Memphis, Tennessee, recently wrote, 'The taxes that are taken out of my check is money that I need, not extra play money. Please do all that you can to make the tax system more equitable toward the family.' Well, sir, that's just what we intend to do—to pass the strongest pro-family initiative in postwar history."

Putting himself on the side of struggling families, Reagan explained his simplification plan as a boon to the vast majority of Americans. Even the deduction for state and local taxes, he argued, had been a "special subsidy for high-income individuals, especially in a few high-tax states." The elimination of such deductions would be, he said, a victory for fairness.

The tax system required change, he said, because of changing times and conditions. With a smile beginning to form on his lips, he said that comparing the current tax code with his new plan would be like comparing a Model T to the space shuttle. "And I should know," he said, "I've seen both."

"This, then, is our plan—America's tax plan, a revolutionary first for fairness in our future, a long overdue commitment to help working Americans and their families, and a challenge to our entire nation to excel … My fellow citizens, let's not let this magnificent moment slip away. Tax relief is in sight. Let's make it a reality. Let's not let prisoners of mediocrity wear us down. Let's not let the special interest raids of the few rob us of all our dreams … We can do it. And if you help, we will do it this year."

It was a stirring appeal, and perhaps to his surprise, Democrats treated it with respect and they, too, spoke of the importance of fairness and opportunity, and one prominent Democrat, Senator Bill Bradley of New Jersey, became a prominent champion of tax simplification. But Reagan's hope that the bill would pass in 1985 was not to be. The plan stalled in part over the president's elimination of deductions for state and local tax cuts. Republicans and Democrats from high-tax states joined together to fight the president, and when tax reform eventually made its way to the president's desk, the deduction remained intact.

Reagan did not get everything he wanted, but the tax reform of 1986 remains one of his administration's most prominent domestic achievements. Reagan later wrote that between the tax cuts of 1981 and tax reform in 1986, "I'd accomplished a lot of what I'd come to Washington to do."[4]

But his second term was only just beginning.

A strange plume of flame is seen on the right side of the rocket booster of the space shuttle Challenger *shortly after liftoff; seconds later, the shuttle exploded*

CHAPTER 22

The *Challenger* Disaster

Address to the Nation
January 28, 1986

TRACK 22

THE YEAR 1986 FIGURED TO BE A PIVOTAL TWELVE MONTHS FOR RONALD Reagan. Midterm elections beckoned—the last of his administration—and soon all eyes would begin to look ahead to the presidential campaign of 1988. As a lame duck, Reagan's power to cajole and persuade Congress and the public was diminishing with each passing month. It was time to use up every bit of political capital in order to make the Reagan Revolution permanent.

Mid-January found Reagan and his staff working on his annual State of the Union message, scheduled for Tuesday night, January 28. Domestic issues would dominate the president's themes again, particularly tax reform, but Reagan would also acknowledge a planned visit later in the year by the Soviet Union's leader, Mikhail Gorbachev. The visit grew out of a summit meeting between the two leaders in Geneva in late 1985, the first such U.S.-Soviet meeting of the Reagan years.

During the summit, as aides to the two leaders sparred over arms control during a formal negotiating session, Reagan asked Gorbachev to join him for a walk outside, just the two of them and their translators—a seemingly spontaneous gesture that, in fact, White House staff had planned. The two leaders strolled near Lake Geneva, chatted about movies, and then continued their conversation in front of a fireplace in a pool house near the lake. Reagan showed Gorbachev a document that included an American proposal to reduce its nuclear force by 50 percent. The Soviet leader was impressed, the two men kept talking, and a historic relationship was born. When the summit drew to a close, Reagan rejected tough language inserted into his remarks by speechwriters Pat Buchanan and Peggy Noonan. He told Buchanan, "Pat, this has been a good meeting. I think I can work with this guy."[1] The public understood that something extraordinary was unfolding before their eyes—Reagan's approval ratings skyrocketed.

While Reagan was being hailed for his statesmanship, his domestic program remained a serious source of contention between the White House and the Democratic leadership in the House. While the economy was growing and fortunes were being made in the financial services sector, blue-collar jobs continued to disappear, and unemployment, while better than it was when Reagan entered office, was at 7 percent, distressingly high at a time when many Americans were doing well. With the House up for reelection in November, Reagan could expect intensified attacks from Democrats who portrayed him as insensitive to the needs of the poor and unemployed.

Perhaps anticipating those criticisms, Reagan used his weekly radio address on Saturday, January 25, to make a pitch for cooperation. He noted that he was due to deliver his annual State of the Union speech in three days, and then added, as a "piece of trivia," that Woodrow Wilson revived the idea of delivering the annual message in person rather than sending it in writing to Congress, a tradition started by Thomas Jefferson. Reagan quoted from Wilson's explanation for why he wished to speak directly to Congress: "I'm very glad to have this opportunity to address the two Houses directly and to verify for myself that the president is a person, not a mere department of the government hailing Congress from some isolated island of jealous power—that he is a human being trying to cooperate with other human beings in a common service."

Reagan lingered on Wilson's sentiments. "Cooperate in a common service," he repeated, "I guess that pretty much says it all."[2] It did, in fact, say a great deal about Reagan's conception of power: as he demonstrated during the Geneva summit, Reagan was a firm believer in personal contact, in the interaction of human beings "trying to cooperate with other human beings." That was why he asked Gorbachev to take a walk. He earnestly believed that sincere people could straighten out the differences in the greater interest of humanity.

The problem was that not everybody was susceptible to charm, or even sincerity. On the morning of January 28, the president met with Speaker O'Neill and other Congressional leaders to talk about the State of the Union speech to be delivered later that night. In discussing the economy, Reagan told the congressional leaders that, in essence, unemployment was not as bad a problem as it was being made out to be. Not for the first time, the president told a story of an unemployed man who refused to accept a job offer. The story proved, Reagan said, that some of the unemployed simply didn't want to work.

According to an account of the meeting in Lou Cannon's book, *President Reagan: The Role of a Lifetime*, O'Neill erupted. "Don't give me that crap," he said, according to Cannon. "The guy in Youngstown, Ohio, who'd been laid off at the steel mill and has to make his mortgage payments—don't tell me he doesn't want to work. Those stories may work on your rich friends, but they don't work on the rest of us. I'm sick and tired of your attitude, Mr. President."3

Republican Senator Alan Simpson of Wyoming quickly interjected himself into the tense standoff between Reagan and O'Neill, and the Speaker quickly explained that he meant no disrespect to the presidency. "With the exception of this incumbent," Reagan snapped back, unwilling to accept O'Neill's apology. The president was angry not only over O'Neill's outburst, but over repeated Democratic charges that he was heartless and unsympathetic. What the Democrats didn't understand, Cannon wrote, was Reagan's sincerity. He believed his policies were working, and he believed he had the evidence on his side. In his own account of the meeting, Reagan wrote simply that he "had a few words with Tip O'Neill."4

As tempers flared in Washington, seven Americans were preparing for the trip of a lifetime in Florida. They were the crew of the space shuttle *Challenger*, and after waiting through several delays in their planned mission they once again were scheduled for liftoff that morning. The shuttle flights had become so routine that they were almost nonevents; only the somewhat new cable network, CNN, chose to televise the launch, even though the *Challenger* mission featured a much publicized twist. One of its crew members was a schoolteacher named Christa McAuliffe, who was chosen to fly into space as part of NASA's new Teacher in Space program. McAuliffe, a thirty-seven-year-old mother of two grade-school children, was one of eleven thousand teachers who applied for the program. Reagan met with McAuliffe in late 1985 as part of the publicity buildup for the launch.

It was a cold morning at the Kennedy Space Center in Florida Nighttime temperatures sank below freezing, forcing teams of NASA workers to remove ice that formed on the shuttle on the launch pad. Mechanical troubles prompted delays and the launch was pushed back to around 11:30 a.m. while the crews finished the job.

Across the country, teachers stopped their lesson plans and routines as liftoff approached. McAuliffe's presence on the shuttle meant that millions of schoolchildren and teachers felt they were a part of the mission, and part of history, as well.

The rocket ignited at 11:38 a.m., emitting great plumes of white smoke as it lifted the shuttle away from earth. Thousands on hand to witness the launch firsthand burst into applause.

In Washington, Reagan was at his desk in the Oval Office, meeting with press spokesman Larry Speakes about the State of the Union speech. The president did not watch the launch.

The launch appeared to be routinely perfect. The rocket headed skyward, twenty-thousand, thirty-thousand, forty-thousand feet into the air, now barely visible from the ground. But a vital component called an O-ring, which prevented hot gasses from leaking out of a rocket booster, was failing, in part because of the effects of the cold temperature at liftoff. About a minute into the flight, flames began to appear outside the rocket near a damaged joint. The shuttle began to disintegrate. It broke apart in a cloud of white vapor seventy-three seconds into the flight. The shuttle's cabin, where McAuliffe and her colleagues were stationed, plummeted back to earth and crashed into the Atlantic Ocean.

Moments later, Vice President George Bush and several aides entered the Oval Office unannounced to tell Reagan what had happened. He put his face in his hands.

The seven crew members—McAuliffe, Michael J. Smith, Commander Dick Scobee, Ronald McNair, Ellison Onizuka, Gregory Jarvis, and Judith Resnik—were dead. Classrooms across the nation were in shock, teachers too numb to try to explain what their students just witnessed. It was the nation's worst space disaster since a fire on the ground killed the crew of Apollo 1 in 1967.

Reagan turned on a television in an adjoining room to monitor coverage of the disaster. He stood, grim-faced, and watched replays of the awful images from the blue Florida sky. Patrick Buchanan, arms folded and head down, stood to his left, and to Buchanan's left was Chief of Staff Donald Regan, his left hand clutching a briefing book. A little more than an hour later, Reagan met with reporters in the Roosevelt Room at 1:00 p.m. for a previous scheduled briefing about the State of the Union message. All of the questions, however, were about *Challenger*. Asked about any "special thoughts" he had about McAuliffe, Reagan said that he couldn't "get out of my mind" thoughts about her husband and children. Knowing "that they were there [in Florida] and watching," he said, "this just is—well, your heart goes out to them."

Reagan indicated that he would deliver his State of the Union message as planned later that evening, explaining that "you can't stop governing the nation because of a tragedy of this kind. So, yes, we'll continue."5

He and his staff changed their minds soon afterwards. The message was postponed. Instead, Reagan delivered a short speech on national television about the tragedy. He went on the air at five o'clock, waiting until the fate of the crew members was certain. Once again, the speech was the work of Peggy Noonan.

He announced that the State of the Union was postponed. "Today is a day for mourning and remembering," he said. "This is truly a national loss."

He mentioned the crew members by name. "For the families of the seven," he said, "we cannot bear, as you do, the full impact of this tragedy. But we feel the loss, and we're thinking about you so very much. Your loved ones were daring and brave, and they had that special grace, that special spirit that says, 'Give me a challenge, and I'll meet it with joy.' They had a hunger to explore the universe and discover its truths. They wished to serve, and they did. They served all of us. We've grown used to wonders in this century. It's hard to dazzle us. But for 25 years the United States space program has been doing just that. We've grown used to the idea of space, and perhaps we forget that we've only just begun. We're still pioneers."

But surely there were some Americans for whom space travel was fresh and exciting, who had been prepared to witness the flight of a teacher into space, symbolizing the nation's commitment to education, and to the future. They were, of course, America's schoolchildren. They were too young to be weary of adventure. Their eyes were new, their perspective fresh. And on this day in January, they had witnessed catastrophe.

Reagan addressed them directly. "I know it is hard to understand," he said, "but sometimes painful things like this happen. It's all part of the process of exploration and discovery. It's all part of taking a chance and expanding man's horizons. The future doesn't belong to the fainthearted; it belongs to the brave. The *Challenger* crew was pulling us into the future, and we'll continue to follow them."

Reagan saw the space program as a historic adventure, with Americans leading the way with know-how and courage. For that reason, he said, the disaster would not be a barrier to more exploration, more discovery. "We'll continue our quest in space," he said. "There will be more shuttle flights and more shuttle crews and, yes, more volunteers, more civilians, more teachers in space. Nothing ends here; our hopes and our journeys continue."

Reagan closed with a two phrases from a poem written by a young World War II pilot, John Magee, who was killed in action at the age of nine-teen. As Reagan biographer Richard Reeves noted, Reagan knew the quote. His friend and fellow actor, Tyrone Power, had carried the verse with him during his own service in the U.S. Air Force. [6]

"The crew of the space shuttle *Challenger* honored us by the manner in which they lived their lives," he said. "We will never forget them, not the last time we saw them, this morning, as they prepared for their journey and waved goodbye and 'slipped the surly bonds of earth' to touch 'the face of God.'"

The *Challenger* speech remains one of Reagan's best-remembered per-formances. Tip O'Neill, who had quarreled so bitterly with Reagan earlier that morning, later wrote: "It was a trying day for all Americans, and Ronald Reagan spoke to our highest ideals."[7]

The Reagans attend a memorial service with the families of the Challenger *victims*

Muammar al-Qaddafi addresses a rally at Martyrs' Square in Tripoli, Libya

CHAPTER 23

The Shores of Tripoli

Address to the Nation
Following a U.S. Air Strike on Libya
April 14, 1986

TRACK 23

O N THE MORNING OF DECEMBER 27, 1985, THOUSANDS OF TRAVELERS WERE waiting to board their planes in Vienna International Airport in Austria and in Rome's Leonardo da Vinci Airport. At just after eight o'clock, four men approached the counter of El Al Airlines, the national carrier of Israel, in da Vinci airport. Suddenly, the men began shooting passengers with assault rifles. One or more of the assailants hurled grenades into the crowd. At about the same time, in Vienna, three men near the El Al counter tossed hand grenades at passengers waiting for a flight to Israel. The waiting area was turned into a slaughterhouse.

The airport attacks of December 27 killed eighteen people, including several Americans and a child, and wounded nearly a hundred and fifty. Authorities in Rome killed three of the attackers there and captured one, while in Austria the police killed one attacker and captured the other two after they tried to escape by car.

The murderous attack shocked Europe and the United States. Although suspicion fell on the Palestine Liberation Organization, U.S. intelligence reported that Colonel Qaddafi, the military leader of Libya, was behind the attacks. The Reagan administration already had crossed swords with Libya, when two U.S. warplanes shot down a pair of Libyan fighters over the Gulf of Sidra in 1981. It had been monitoring Qaddafi's activities since the incident. Evidence was mounting that the Libyan leader was financing and equipping terrorists who were attacking Western interests in the Middle East and beyond.

Reagan met with his national security advisors on January 7. He decided to cut any remaining economic ties to the country and ordered any Americans living in the country to come home. The Sixth Fleet, based in the Mediterranean Sea, would move into the Gulf of Sidra to conduct maneuvers. In his diary, Reagan wrote, "If Mr. Qaddafi decided not to push another terrorist act, okay, we've been successful with our implied threat." If, however, Qaddafi persisted, Reagan wrote, "we will have targets in mind."[1]

The Sixth Fleet was waiting to see what Qaddafi would do next, if anything. But it was hardly passive. Navy warplanes patrolled the area and several ships intentionally crossed what Qaddafi called a "line of death" close to the shoreline. Libyan guns opened fire on the U.S. planes on March 24, but they didn't come close to hitting their targets. The following day, a U.S. warplane attacked and destroyed a Libyan vessel as it neared the American warships. More skirmishes followed.

America's allies in Europe followed events in the Mediterranean with growing anxiety. More dependent on Arab oil, including oil from Libya, and closer geographically to the Arab-Islamic world, Europe was reluctant to confront Qaddafi, even though the attacks he allegedly sponsored took place on European, not American, soil. All the while, U.S. intelligence was intercepting communications from Tripoli, the Libyan capital, urging operatives abroad to attack American targets.

Reagan and his wife were in California for a short vacation at his ranch when, on April 5, a bomb blast ripped through a nightclub in West Berlin known as a popular spot for U.S. soldiers. One U.S. soldier was killed, as was a civilian. More than one hundred and fifty people were hurt.

Qaddafi condemned the attack, but Reagan and his aides were sifting through intercepted communications between Tripoli and Libya's embassy in East Berlin. The evidence, Reagan wrote, "established conclusively" that Libya was behind the attack. The intercepts also tipped off U.S. intelligence about other planned attacks.[2]

Reagan returned to Washington to preside over a meeting to discuss how and when the United States would retaliate. Listening to intelligence reports about Qaddafi's behavior and his supposed taste for women's clothes, Reagan decided that his antagonist was "not only a barbarian, he's flaky."3 As for the report about Qaddafi's wardrobe, Reagan said, "Maybe we could stop the terror by letting him into Nancy's closet."4

While few doubted that the United States would strike Libya, Reagan allowed time to pass while he and his aides reviewed plans and contacted allies. On April 9, at a planned presidential news conference, Reagan was bombarded with questions about Libya, beginning with an opening query from the dean of the White House press corps, Helen Thomas of United Press International. If the president was "contemplating major retaliation," Thomas asked, "won't you be killing a lot of innocent people?" Reagan ignored Thomas's question about innocents caught in the line of fire, and said simply that "any action that we might take would be dependent on what we learn." Another reporter asked Reagan what "precautions" Americans might take "to prevent terrorist attacks at home." Reagan said that U.S. intelligence already had "aborted 126 planned terrorist attacks that never took place because of our having information in advance."5

As the days wore on, some news organizations reported that the United States was planning a strike against Qaddafi, which enraged Reagan although it could hardly have surprised the Libyan leader. "I really lost my patience with the press," Reagan wrote in his autobiography.6

But reporters were not the only players who were proving difficult to manage. The emerging U.S. plan of attack called for the deployment of F-111 heavy bombers based in Britain, but the governments of Italy and France refused to allow the bombers to fly over their national air space. They would have to veer west, over the eastern Atlantic, to get to their targets. Reagan had another reason to lose his patience. Years later, he accused France of "trying to play both sides" in the dispute.7

The attack began at two o'clock in the morning on April 15, seven o'clock in Washington. The F-111 bombers attacked targets in Tripoli, while carrier-based planes bombed Benghazi. The attack on Tripoli just missed Qaddafi, but killed his adopted daughter, who was just over a year old, and wounded two of his sons. One of the U.S. missiles went astray and slammed into a residential area of the city, killing civilians. Fireballs lit up the desert sky as the American warplanes made their getaway.

Libyan antiaircraft fire, streaks of red light shooting through the night, may have claimed one of the F-111 bombers. It crashed, killing two crewmen.

At nine o'clock eastern time that night, just two hours after the attacks were carried out, Reagan spoke to the nation in a televised address. He announced that "air and naval forces" had carried out "a series of strikes" against Qaddafi's "headquarters, terrorist facilities, and military assets." The attacks, he said, had "succeeded."

The purpose of his speech was not to lead cheers for the military, nor was it to outline in detail what had taken place only hours earlier, thousands of miles away. Rather, he was intent on justifying his actions. To that end, he noted that he had warned Qaddafi that he would be held accountable "for any new terrorist attacks launched against American citizens." That attack came in West Berlin, and Reagan told the American people there was little doubt who had planned it. "Libya's agents … planted the bomb," he said. On April 4, the country's embassy in East Berlin "alerted Tripoli that the attack would be carried out the following morning. The next day they reported back to Tripoli on the great success of their mission."

While Reagan's prime audience was the American public, he also had a message for other nations: they, too, had much to fear from Qaddafi, even if he had chosen to target Americans in his most recent attack.

"Colonel Qaddafi is not only an enemy of the United States," Reagan said. "His record of subversion and aggression against the neighboring states in Africa is well documented and well known … He has sanctioned acts of terror in Africa, Europe, and the Middle East, as well as the Western Hemisphere. Today we have done what we had to do. If necessary, we shall do it again. It gives me no pleasure to say that, and I wish it were otherwise."

There were others who wished it were otherwise, but they were unwilling to realize that they could not simply wish away a problem like Qaddafi. Reagan directed his message to his European critics, who were even then issuing statements condemning the American action.

"Europeans who remember history understand better than most that there is no security, no safety, in the appeasement of evil," he said. "It must be the core of Western policy that there be no sanctuary for terror. And to sustain such a policy, free men and free nations must unite and work together. Sometimes it is said that by imposing sanctions against Colonel Qaddafi or by striking at his terrorist installations we only magnify the man's importance, that the proper way to deal with him is to ignore him. I do not agree."

Americans were "slow to anger," he said, but in this case, their anger was justified, and their methods were in keeping with principles of self-defense. Qaddafi had calculated that he could attack with impunity. "He counted on America to be passive," he said. "He counted wrong."

"I warned that there should be no place on Earth where terrorists can rest and train and practice their deadly skills," he said. "I meant it. I said that we would act with others, if possible, and alone if necessary to ensure that terrorists have no sanctuary anywhere. Tonight, we have."

The speech, along with the mission's success, was an overwhelming success. Polls put Reagan's approval ratings at around 70 percent. Newspapers rallied around him, persuaded by his evidence that Libya was behind the bombing, convinced that Qaddafi had to be punished severely.

"After the attack on Tripoli," Reagan wrote with some satisfaction, "we didn't hear much more from Qaddafi's terrorists."

But the turbulent region in which Qaddafi operated would continue to bedevil Reagan and his aides.

Nancy Reagan speaks at a "Just Say No" rally in Los Angeles, California

CHAPTER 24

Just Say No

Address by President and
Nancy Reagan about Drug Abuse
September 14, 1986

TRACK 24

IN HIS AUTOBIOGRAPHY, RONALD REAGAN WROTE THAT HIS LIFE "REALLY BEGAN" when he met a film actress named Nancy Davis.[1] They were introduced in the early 1950s, when Reagan was president of the Screen Actors Guild. The actress happened to be one of several women named Nancy Davis working in Hollywood, and one of them apparently was involved in Communist front groups. The future Nancy Reagan was receiving mail from the front groups and was worried about her reputation. Director Mervyn LeRoy called Reagan and asked him to reassure the actress. Take her out to dinner, LeRoy said.

Reagan, single again since his divorce from Jane Wyman in 1948, decided that the prospect of dinner with a young actress was not particularly unpleasant. In fact, it was all in a day's work for the president of the Screen Actors Guild. He wouldn't admit it at the time, but he was lonely after his divorce.

Reagan showed up to Davis's apartment that night leaning on two canes. He broke his thighbone while playing in a charity softball game weeks earlier, and the injury still hadn't healed properly. If he didn't sweep Nancy Davis off her feet that night, perhaps it was because his arms were otherwise occupied.

They began dating casually, then more seriously, and on March 4, 1952, Ronald Reagan and Nancy Davis were married in a private ceremony, with William Holden and his wife Ardis as the only witnesses other than the presiding clergyman.

The bond between Ronald and Nancy Reagan was extraordinary. Neither show business nor politics is known for the stability of its marriages, but as the years passed, the Reagans seemed to grow closer. She was fiercely protective of him; he was passionately loyal to her, and called her "Mommy." They shunned the glamorous life that might have been theirs. Instead, they retreated to a small world they created for themselves and a few friends. They preferred their own company, just the two of them, to the nightlife and socializing that was so much a part of the Hollywood life. "Nancy and I," Reagan wrote, never did "much partying in Hollywood— our idea of an exciting evening was to spend it at home with the children."[2]

Together, they had Patti and Ronald Jr., to go along with Maureen and Michael, Reagan's children with Jane Wyman. But if Reagan portrayed his home life as idyllic, with mom and dad home on a regular basis, reality was more complex, as it generally is with families. His daughter Maureen was estranged from Nancy and would be for years to come. Patti changed her last name to her mother's maiden name, lived the life of a California bohemian even as her father campaigned against the 1960s counterculture, and, during her father's White House years, joined the nuclear-freeze movement to protest her father's deployment of intermediate-range nuclear weapons in Europe.

Through it all, Ron and Nancy offered each other love and companionship that made their other relationships seem fleeting and perhaps even unimportant. They famously let very few people into their world—Reagan biographer Richard Reeves noted that for all the president's personal charm and self-confidence, he had "few if any deep friendships."[3]

If so, he didn't seem bothered. He always had Nancy, and Nancy always had him.

When they left Hollywood for Sacramento after Reagan's election as governor in 1966, they remained aloof from the capital's rounds of fundraising parties and other social engagements. Legislators complained that the Reagans were snobs—more often than not, blame was fixed on Nancy rather than on her seemingly outgoing husband. Nothing could have been further from the truth, but most legislators didn't realize that the man who so enjoyed performing in public, who seemed so comfortable on the campaign trail, was not necessarily the real Ronald Reagan. He was home, with Nancy, in the house they rented because Nancy refused to live in the dilapidated governor's mansion. After dinner, they watched television together in the couple's bedroom, because the governor liked to lay down and relax while watching his favorite variety shows (Dean Martin and Carol Burnett were favorites) and football games.

Accustomed as she was to performance herself, Nancy Reagan played the role of dutiful spouse who supported the Great Man as he made history. But beyond the public performance, Nancy Reagan was a formidable power in her own right. When her husband's campaign was in turmoil in New Hampshire in early 1980, she called William Clark, an old Reagan ally in California, to recruit him as the campaign's chief of staff. She formed a close relationship with Michael Deaver, the president's advisor and image-maker, although that friendship didn't stop her from lashing out at Deaver after her husband's poor performance during his first presidential debate with Walter Mondale in 1984. Those whom she didn't like fared a good deal worse. Secretary of State Alexander Haig and Chief of Staff Donald Regan both ran afoul of the first lady—Haig during Reagan's first term, Regan during the second. Both found themselves out of a job.

Many observers and White House staff concluded that Nancy was a controlling influence on the president. The public saw glimpses of her influence, such as the time, in 1984, when the president was asked what the United States could do to resume arms-control talks with the Soviets. When Reagan seemed at a loss for words, and as network news cameras captured the moment, Nancy, who was standing nearby, whispered the words, "doing everything we can." The president repeated the phrase for the cameras. Reagan's critics seized on the moment to portray Nancy as a sort of shadow president, but Reeves concluded otherwise. Reagan depended on his wife's love and loyalty, Reeves wrote, but he was not her puppet. On several occasions, Reeves noted, the president was overheard saying, in a louder voice than he used in most of his speeches, "That's enough, Nancy!"[4]

For Nancy Reagan, the defining moment of the Reagan administration came very early—March 30, 1981, when John Hinckley very nearly murdered her husband. She was convinced that there would be further attempts on his life, and one of them would succeed. Those fears led her to consult an astrologer, Joan Quigley, about the president's schedules. Reagan's calendar, including proposed meetings with foreign dignitaries, was sometimes adjusted according to Quigley's reading of the stars. Chief of staff Donald Regan had a color-coded calendar on his desk indicating which days were considered good for meetings, and which days weren't. Such was Nancy Reagan's power, and Joan Quigley's.

When Regan wrote about Nancy and astrology in a bitter tell-all memoir of the Reagan White House, the president stood by his woman. The assassination attempt, he explained, had left her fearful about the future. He insisted that astrology did not guide his life, although subsequent revelations suggested otherwise. Years earlier, Reagan supposedly once said that he never made an important decision without consulting the astrology columnist of the *Los Angeles Times*, Carroll Righter. It made perfect sense, for the Reagans shared their lives and interests with each other. If Nancy consulted the stars, it was not hard to believe that her husband did, too.

Nancy Reagan wielded power behind the scenes, far from the prying eyes of the press and voters. But she was not without public influence as well. Early on in her White House years, she adopted the fight against drug abuse as her special cause. Although she could not have known it in 1981, drug abuse took a sinister turn in the middle of the Reagan years when crack cocaine found its way into the streets of America's cities. Cheap and highly addictive, crack would ruin the lives of tens of thousands of mostly young, mostly poor Americans in the mid to late 1980s.

The Reagans themselves were nothing if not a sober couple. As the son of an alcoholic who saw firsthand the effects of addiction, Ronald Reagan was a social drinker at best, and even that description probably exaggerates his use of alcohol. Their personal habits and sense of propriety certainly shielded them from charges of hypocrisy when they warned of the dangers of drugs.

Nancy Reagan toured the country and visited schools to bring home a message she summed up in three words: just say no. If a friend offered you drugs, she said, just say no. For her, and no doubt for her husband, it was that simple. Just say no. Forget peer pressure. Put aside any adolescent longings about acceptance, about fitting in, about wanting to be part of the crowd. Just say no.

Critics charged that resisting drugs wasn't always so simple, but Nancy Reagan's message certainly caught on. It became one of the cultural catchphrases of the era. She served as host for several international conferences about drug abuse and addiction, traveled to dozens of cities throughout the world, and even appeared on the television shows *Dallas* and *Diff'rent Strokes* to deliver her antidrug message.

On the night of September 14, 1986, Ronald Reagan shared his White House stage with Mrs. Reagan as they delivered a nationally televised address about the perils of drug abuse. They had costarred like this only once before, in the war film *Hellcats of the Navy*, released in 1957. The president spoke first, touting his administration's progress in the war on drugs but conceding that "illegal cocaine is coming into our country at alarming levels, and four to five million people regularly use it." Law enforcement alone clearly was not getting the job done. Drug abuse was, at least in the Reagans' view, a moral issue as well.

After brief remarks, the president introduced his wife and costar. It was a historic moment, for no other first lady had ever been given such a powerful platform before. While a generation of first ladies adopted favorite causes, from Lady Bird Johnson's beautification program to Betty Ford's public struggles against alcoholism and breast cancer, they never had the chance to use the president's bully pulpit. Reagan's willingness to share the spotlight with his wife spoke the strength of their bond, and also to his own self-assurance. If Nancy upstaged him, so what?

The First Lady delivered her appeal as a mother, noting that schools around the country were opening their doors for the new academic year. She remembered September as a time of "promise and hope" for the nation's children. But, she said, she could no longer think of September as a time of innocence because, she suggested, drug abuse had stolen the childhoods of so many American youths.

Using language that sounded as foreboding as her husband's when talking about the Soviet threat, Mrs. Reagan said that "so much has happened over these last years, so much to shake the foundations of all that we know and all that we believe in.

"Today," she continued, "there's a drug and alcohol abuse epidemic in this country, and no one is safe from it—not you, not me, and certainly not our children, because this epidemic has their names written on it." Like her husband, Mrs. Reagan used the second person—you—to foster a sense of intimacy with her audience, to persuade the public that she understood its concerns. "Many of you may be thinking: 'Well, drugs don't concern me.' But it does concern you. It concerns us all because of the way it tears at our lives and because it's aimed at destroying the brightness and life of the sons and daughters of the United States."

Mrs. Reagan did not exaggerate the impact of drugs in the mid-1980s. Just three months earlier, the nation was stunned when college basketball star Len Bias died at the age of twenty-two, two days after he was the second selection in the National Basketball Association's annual draft of college players. Bias died of a heart attack brought on by an overdose of cocaine. Public opinion polls showed that drug abuse was a major concern of voters as they began to think about the 1986 midterm elections, and the White House hoped to capitalize on those concerns. The joint appearance by President Reagan and the First Lady was the culmination of Mrs. Reagan's tireless efforts to combat drug abuse, but it also served a political purpose—Republicans were hoping to capitalize on the issue in November in their effort to keep control of the U.S. Senate.

Mrs. Reagan spoke of children, even infants, who were suffering the effects of parental drug abuse. And just as her husband told his evangelical audience in 1983 that they should not search for a middle ground in the struggle against an "evil empire," Mrs. Reagan insisted that the American people could not be mere spectators in this struggle closer to home. "There's no moral middle ground," she said. "Indifference is not an option … For the sake of our children, I implore each of you to be unyielding and inflexible in your opposition to drugs."

Two days after the Reagans spoke, Chief of Staff Donald Regan reported that reaction was overwhelmingly positive. He told speechwriter Kenneth Khachigian, who wrote the script for both President Reagan and the First Lady, that "all reviews are outstanding" and that "never have reactions to one of the president's speeches been more favorable!"[5] Those favorable reactions, however, did not translate into political support in November. Despite Reagan's work on behalf of Republican senate candidates, four Republican incumbents lost their seats, and Democrats seized control of the upper chambers with fifty-five seats. For the first time in the Reagan presidency, Democrats were in charge of both houses of Congress.

With scandal around the corner, the next few months would prove to be the most difficult of Reagan's presidency.

Nancy Reagan with children at a "Just Say No" event at the White House

Ronald Reagan with Adolfo Calero—a Nicaraguan Democratic Resistance (Contra) leader—and Oliver North, a member of the National Security Council staff

CHAPTER 25

Iran-Contra

Address to the Nation
March 4, 1987

TRACK 25

THE ROOTS OF WHAT BECAME KNOWN AS THE IRAN-CONTRA SCANDAL CAN BE traced to the very beginnings of the Reagan administration, or, in fact, to the last year of Jimmy Carter's administration. The hostage crisis in Iran dominated Carter's final year in office and helped lead to his defeat in 1980, but the episode did not truly end with the release of the hostages on January 20, 1981. The legacy of the crisis, the lingering images of American impotence in the face of provocation animated the Reagan administration's policy in the Middle East. Reagan did not want his administration symbolically held hostage by actual hostage taking in the Arab world. But as terrorist groups began kidnapping Americans in the region, Reagan learned, as Carter did before him, the limits of U.S. power in a dangerous world. And his sympathy for the hostages and their families clouded his judgment and did, in the end, seize control of U.S. policy.

In July 1986, President Reagan underwent surgery to remove cancerous polyps in his colon. As he lay in a hospital bed in Bethesda Medical Center in Maryland on July 17, the president noted that the United States was picking up some back-channel "soundings" from Iran. "Bud M. will be here tomorrow to talk about it," he wrote. "It could be a breakthrough on getting our seven kidnap victims back. Evidently the Iranian economy is disintegrating fast under the strain of war."[1] Bud M. was Bud McFarlane, Reagan's national security adviser, who had been dreaming of a diplomatic opening with Iran since the early days of the Reagan administration, when the hostage crisis was a fresh and bitter memory. The kidnap victims to whom Reagan referred had been seized in Lebanon in 1985 and '86. Although the Reagan administration did not allow the hostages to dominate the news or their public statements about Middle Eastern policy, the president himself was intent on winning their release, somehow, some way. "He wanted to get the hostages out," said Secretary of State George Shultz, years later. Shultz said that many White House staff members knew that Reagan "had a soft spot for the hostages. And they exploited him."[2]

McFarlane went to Reagan's bedside on July 18 to brief him on signals he was receiving from Iranian sources that suggested, through an Israeli middleman, that they might be helpful in winning the release of the American hostages in Lebanon. In return for their intervention, the Iranians said they wanted arms, specifically, TOW antitank missiles for use in their bloody, bitter war with Saddam Hussein's Iraq. Reagan seemed intrigued. According to Reagan biographer Richard Reeves, McFarlane mentioned that the arms sales could be illegal under U.S. law. Reagan, according to Reeves' account, replied, "I'm not put off by the idea." He told McFarlane to tell his contacts that "we want to talk with them, we want to exchange ideas, and we'll work toward the day when our confidence with each other can grow."[3]

Later that summer, Israel secretly agreed to sell Iran nearly a hundred TOW missiles, with the understanding that the United States would, in turn, replenish Israel's arsenal. Ironically, some of the weapons shipped to Iran had Hebrew lettering on them. The arms landed in Teheran in late August. Meanwhile, a member of the National Security Council staff, Colonel Oliver North, traveled to Europe under a false name to begin arranging for the expected release of Americans held captive in Lebanon. None, however, was released until the United States agreed to sell the Iranians—through Israel—another four hundred missiles in mid-September.

Reagan would always insist that he did not trade arms for hostages, that, in fact, he tried to create an atmosphere for improved relations with Iran once the Islamic Revolution's spiritual leader, Ayatollah Ruhollah Khomeini, died—he was eighty-five years old in 1985. But his intense interest in freeing the hostages was well known in the White House, as Shultz pointed out.

Secret arms shipments continued in the fall of 1985, but only one hostage was released. In December, as McFarlane prepared to step down as national security adviser, North told a delegation of Israelis about plans to sell arms directly to Iran and to use money from the sales to buy weapons for the Contras, another favorite cause of the president's. Under federal law sponsored by Congressman Edward Boland of Massachusetts, the United States was barred from providing military aid to the Contras, although Congress would soon approve $100 million in nonmilitary aid to the group. North and others saw the secret Iranian arms deals as a backdoor plan to secretly arm the rebels in Nicaragua.

More arms were delivered to Iran in early 1986. That spring, McFarlane and North traveled to Iran on a covert mission to win release of all U.S. hostages, but they achieved no breakthroughs. In fact, while three hostages would be released before news of the arms shipments became public, three more were taken. The transaction was completely one-sided: Iran got the arms it wanted, but Reagan did not achieve his goal of freeing all Americans held prisoner in the Middle East.

In November 1986, after the release of a third hostage, a magazine in Lebanon reported that the United States had sent weapons to Iran in exchange for hostages. Iran then confirmed that McFarlane had visited Teheran as part of the arms trade and hostage negotiation. The country was outraged. Reagan had fostered a tough-guy image in his dealings with the Middle East, encouraging Americans to believe that he was not the type who negotiated with terrorists, as he showed with Colonel Qaddafi. The very notion of his administration bargaining for hostages, and with Iran, no less, seemed to betray Reagan's own rhetoric and beliefs.

The uproar angered Reagan, who blamed the public's reaction on the press. "The media looks like it's trying to create another Watergate," he wrote in his diary.[4] He decided to address the country in a prime-time broadcast on November 13, just a few days after midterm elections produced a Democratic majority in the Senate. "We did not, repeat, did not trade weapons or anything else for hostages, nor will we," he said.[5] Meanwhile, Oliver North and his assistants were destroying documents that might have revealed more details not only about the Iranian weapons deal, but another component of the plan: money, and arms, for the Contras. The president learned on November 24 that one important document escaped North's shredders: a memo noting that North had diverted some of the profits from the Iranian sales to the Contras—with the approval of John Poindexter, McFarlane's successor as national security adviser.

Reagan's cabinet was in disarray. Both Secretary of State George Shultz and Secretary of Defense Caspar Weinberger had opposed the dealings with Iran. Now, Shultz threatened to leave unless Reagan fired Poindexter. Reagan agreed. "This may call for resignations," the president wrote in his diary.[6]

So it did. Poindexter resigned, North was fired, and Reagan told the country of the Contra piece to the developing scandal. He asked a special investigative committee, to be chaired by former Texas Senator John Tower, to look into the affair.

The next few months were the worst of Reagan's tenure. William Casey resigned as head of the CIA and died soon after of a brain tumor. Bud McFarlane attempted suicide on the eve of a planned appearance before the Tower Commission. Nancy Reagan led a furious and not-very-secret campaign to oust Donald Regan as chief of staff. She blamed him for the blowup over Iran-Contra.

Reagan himself appeared before the Tower committee twice, leaving investigators with an impression that he simply didn't know what was going on in the White House. He read from notes, but seemed confused and unsure of himself. The commission made its findings public on February 26. It painted a picture of a chaotic administration, led by an out-of-touch chief executive. But while it blamed Reagan for the overall dysfunction, it did not find that he was responsible for the Iran-Contra operation. "The president clearly did not understand the nature of this operation," Tower said.[7]

Regan resigned in late February, bitter about the way he was treated in his final few weeks in office and well aware that Nancy Reagan led the campaign against him.

Former Tennessee Senator Howard Baker replaced him as Washington buzzed about the First Lady's influence over the administration.

With the release of the Tower report and its unflattering picture of the Reagan White House, pressure mounted on Reagan to explain himself, in his own words, to the American people. On March 4, the president delivered a nationally televised address that would test his reputation as a great communicator. The daily drumbeat of news stories and revelations called into question his administration's competency and the president's abilities. Reagan always looked and acted like a much younger man, but in the throes of a major scandal, he suddenly looked like the seventy-six-year-old man he was.

He started speaking at nine o'clock from the Oval Office, and made explicit reference to the office in his opening remarks. "The power of the presidency is often thought to reside within this Oval Office," he said. "Yet it doesn't rest here; it rests in you, the American people, and in your trust. Your trust is what gives a president his powers of leadership and his personal strength, and it's what I want to talk to you about this evening."

It was a candid acknowledgment of the president's dilemma in late winter 1987. Reagan was proud of his relationship with the American people, a relationship that was built on the perception that he was not just another politician. But something had gone terribly wrong. Not only had the administration sold arms to a regime that so recently had held Americans hostage for more than a year, not only had White House staff illegally diverted funds to aid the Contras, but Reagan had assured the American public in the fall that he had not traded arms for hostages. Now, however, it was clear that the United States had, in fact, done just that.

Reagan had no choice but to concede what the country already knew. His ability to govern during the last two years of his administration depended on how he managed his concession, and how the American public responded.

"A few months ago," Reagan said, "I told the American people I did not trade arms for hostages. My heart and my best intentions still tell me that's true, but the facts and the evidence tell me it is not. As the Tower board reported, what began as a strategic opening to Iran deteriorated, in its implementation, into trading arms for hostages. This runs counter to my own beliefs, to administration policy, and to the original strategy we had in mind." It was, he said, "a mistake." He conceded that he let his "personal concern for the hostages" dictate "geopolitical strategy." In other words, he allowed hostages—and hostage-takers—to seize control of his foreign policy. Just as Jimmy Carter did.

Reagan assured family members of the hostages that he would continue to work for their release. But bitter reality forced him to make an

un-Reagan-like concession. After saying that he would use "every legiti-
mate means" to free the remaining hostages, he said, "But I must also cau-
tion that those Americans who freely remain in such dangerous areas must
know that they're responsible for their own safety."

It was a stern, realistic, and sad admission.

The Tower Report's findings about Iran-Contra were troubling, indeed,
but equally disturbing were the revelations about how the Reagan White
House functioned—or didn't. Reagan had little choice but to address the
commission's explicit criticisms of his White House and leadership style.

"Much has been said about my management style, a style that's worked
successfully for me during eight years as governor of California and for most
of my presidency," he said. He explained that he preferred to hire good people and let them do their job with minimal interference. But, he said, "when it
came to managing the [National Security Council] staff, let's face it, my style
didn't match its previous track record." Bitter concession followed bitter concession: he admitted that he had failed "to recollect" whether he had approved
an arms shipment to Iran when asked about it by the Tower Commission. "I
did approve it," he admitted, "I just can't say specifically when." He blamed his
memory failure on the NSC's failure to keep proper records.

The president's mea culpa was accompanied by announcements
designed to persuade the public that the White House had learned its lesson
and was taking steps in the right directions. Reagan mentioned Howard
Baker's appointment as chief of staff to replace Regan and the naming of
Frank Carlucci to replace John Poindexter as national security advisor. The
previous day, Reagan had nominated William Webster to replace the termi-
nally ill William Casey as director of the CIA.

Investigations into the affair would continue, Reagan conceded. But he
told the nation that the business of the nation would have to continue.
"You know, by the time you reach my age, you've made plenty of mistakes
… You put things in perspective. You pull your energies together. You
change. You go forward."

It would not be so easy. Congressional hearings followed, during which
Oliver North became a celebrity of sorts as he gave his version of events.
Reagan had hardly acknowledged the Contra component of the scandal, but
congressional investigators and the press continued to look into the diver-
sion of money to the Nicaraguan rebels.

Iran-Contra was the bleakest episode of the Reagan years. But from a broader perspective, it was the darkness before dawn, a dawn that would bring an extraordinary change in relations between the United States and the Soviet Union.

Ronald Reagan receives the Tower Commission Report with committee chair Senator John Tower and committee member Edmund Muskie

Ronald Reagan with Mikhail Gorbachev in Reykjavik, Iceland

CHAPTER 26

Tear Down This Wall!

Speech at the Brandenburg Gate, West Berlin
June 12, 1987

TRACK 26

I RAN-CONTRA DID NOT GO AWAY AFTER THE PRESIDENT'S ADDRESS IN MARCH. Washington did not stop whispering about the picture drawn of a disengaged president surrounded by aides who were willing to stretch and even break the law to achieve their ends. Televised congressional hearings dominated the news in the spring of 1987, and while millions of Americans tuned in, Reagan himself made a point of ignoring them.

Behind the scenes, as Iran-Contra dominated the news cycle, Washington and Moscow were engaged in talks aimed at eliminating intermediate-range nuclear weapons in Europe. It was, in fact, the zero option that Reagan advocated during his first term. As the talks progressed, Reagan pushed for a summit meeting with Gorbachev, hoping that such a high-level event might reenergize his administration and, not coincidentally, overshadow the Iran-Contra investigation. Reagan said he hoped a summit would allow the two leaders to "complete an historic agreement on East-West relations."[1] Reagan and Gorbachev had met in Reykjavík, Iceland, in October 1986, for what Reagan believed would be a short planning meeting for a larger arms-control summit later in the year. Reagan arrived in Iceland first, and so was on hand to watch television coverage of Gorbachev's arrival. He was stunned to see Raisa Gorbachev stepping off the plane. Nancy Reagan was home in

Washington, passing up the trip because her husband believed the meeting would be short and limited in scope. Reagan realized that he was at a disadvantage, for Raisa and Mikhail Gorbachev each were impressive in their own right, but were formidable as a team. The Soviet leader's wife was very much Nancy Reagan's counterpart, but Reagan didn't have Nancy in Iceland, and Gorbachev had Raisa.

Before flying to Iceland, Gorbachev tried to get a scouting report about Reagan from French President François Mitterrand. Gorbachev told him that he wanted to get Washington to give up on missile defense, but Mitterrand said Reagan would not concede the point—negotiations premised on American surrender of "Star Wars" were doomed to failure. But Gorbachev ignored Mitterrand's advice, for he shared with his American counterpart an unfailing belief in his own persuasive powers. He opened the meeting with a bold proposal for both sides to cut their strategic arsenals in half. Reagan's team was stunned, and soon there was talk of eliminating all nuclear weapons, but as the sessions wore on, missile defense became the obstacle that Mitterrand predicted. The meetings broke up abruptly, and both men left Iceland weary and frustrated. "I wasn't going to renege on my promises to the American people not to surrender the SDI," Reagan wrote in his autobiography.[2] A historic easing of Cold War tensions seemed within reach, but the leaders and their negotiators seemed to let the moment slip away.

Reagan returned to the United States angry and empty-handed, just as details of the arms sales to Iran became public. For the moment, Soviet-American relations took a back seat as the nation absorbed details of a scandal that threatened to derail Ronald Reagan's presidency.

That threat began to ease in late spring as investigators focused on the actions of underlings like Oliver North and Elliot Abrams, among others. Still, there was no shortage of depressing headlines and public doubts about Reagan's effectiveness in the spring of 1987. Not only was there scandal in the air—former presidential aide Michael Deaver was indicted in March on charges related to his lobbying business—but tragedy as well. In mid-May, the U.S.S. *Stark*, on patrol in the Persian Gulf, was hit by an Iraqi missile that killed more than two dozen sailors. The Iraqis said the strike was an accident, and Reagan seemed to accept their explanation, blaming not the Iraqi dictator, Saddam Hussein, but Iraq's mortal enemy, Iran. The two nations remained locked in a bloody, indecisive war, six years after Iraq invaded Iran. Reagan seemed to suggest that Iraq would not have fired the weapons were it not at war with Iran, so it was Iran's fault.

The president left the country for ten days in mid-June to attend an economic summit in Venice, Italy. Included on the agenda was a post-summit visit to West Berlin to participate in ceremonies marking the 750th anniversary of the founding of the once and future capital of the German state. Reagan saw the Berlin trip as more than just another cere-monial visit. Like John Kennedy before him, he could visit the Berlin wall, the very symbol of East-West divisions, to speak the plain truth about what that wall meant to freedom-loving people around the world.

Speechwriter Peter Robinson was given the assignment of crafting a speech for Reagan's appearance at the wall. Nearly a quarter-century earlier, John F. Kennedy's speechwriters were given a similar assignment, and they drafted a carefully worded, inoffensive statement which Kennedy decided he simply could not deliver, not after he saw his first glimpse of the wall. Instead, Kennedy delivered the angry speech for which he became famous, adding the German phrase Ich bin ein Berliner. No linguist, Kennedy had practiced the line over and over again during his flight across the Atlantic from Washington.

Reagan consciously sought to return to the themes Kennedy sounded in that uncharacteristically raw, passionate speech in 1963. But his advisors were not as eager to embrace confrontational rhetoric even as the United States and Soviets were moving closer to an historic arms-control agree-ment. Ironically, John Kennedy faced the same dilemma himself: his Berlin wall speech came as the Soviets and Americans were working on an historic treaty to outlaw nuclear testing in the atmosphere. After he delivered his speech, in which he criticized those who say "we can work with the Communists," an aide reminded him that his administration was doing just that—working with the Communists in Moscow on a test-ban treaty.

Robinson, Reagan's speechwriter, knew that Reagan wanted to include a line in the speech asking Gorbachev to tear down the Berlin wall. But, according to Reagan biographer Richard Reeves, senior White House offi-cials, including Chief of Staff Howard Baker, were opposed to any such inflammatory rhetoric, in part because it would have put Reagan in the position of asking for the impossible. Reagan, however, insisted. According to Reeves, he asked his speechwriter, "Now, I'm the president, aren't I?" Peter Robinson wisely agreed.

"Well," Reagan said, "the line stays in."3

The president arrived in West Berlin on the morning of June 12. He was scheduled to speak outdoors, as Kennedy did, near the Brandenburg Gate, which was on the East Berlin side of the wall. Before his speech, Reagan met with West German officials in a building that towered over the wall, allowing the president a glimpse into the Soviet-controlled portion of the city. Kennedy, too, had caught a glimpse of life on the other side during his visit: he saw women waving to him, and an aide told him that they risked being shot for their gesture of friendship. He was enraged when he mounted a platform to give what became one of his most famous speeches.

Reagan, in his glimpse of East Berlin, saw police moving citizens away from the wall so that they couldn't hear his speech over loudspeakers. Like Kennedy, he became angry, and brought that anger with him to the podium when it was time to speak.

The Germans constructed a platform in front of the wall, with the Brandenburg Gate looming behind Reagan, the East German flag flying limply atop the gate on a windless spring day. Thousands of West Berliners gathered in front of the platform, and while they were not as numerous nor as raucous as the crowd that welcomed John Kennedy in 1963, their enthusiasm was evident, and astonishing. Only four years earlier, crowds as large as this one, and even larger, filled the streets of Europe's cities not to welcome Ronald Reagan, but to condemn him as a warmonger, a reckless cowboy. The nuclear-freeze movement had its enemy, and it was Ronald Reagan.

Now, with the Soviets and Americans on the verge of a historic arms control agreement, Ronald Reagan was being hailed as a peacemaker.

With his friend Helmut Kohl, the West German chancellor, seated to his left, Reagan began with an explicit reference to Kennedy's visit. "We come to Berlin, we American Presidents, because it's our duty to speak, in this place, of freedom," he said. And just to complete the connection between JFK's visit and his own, Reagan trotted out some German of his own. Addressing himself to "those listening throughout Eastern Europe," he said: "Although I cannot be with you, I address my remarks to you just as surely as to those standing here before me. For I join you, as I join your fellow countrymen in the West, in this firm, this unalterable belief: Es gibt nur ein Berlin." (In English, "There is only one Berlin.")

While Kennedy's performance at the wall was brief, passionate, and seemingly unscripted, Reagan's speech was a set-piece address that elaborated on themes Kennedy touched on in 1963. And while the two speeches were very different in content and style—Kennedy's was a fierce, emotional protest; Reagan's was a carefully constructed argument—they both drew on the decades of German-American friendship that followed two horrific wars during which the United States and Germany were enemies.

"In this season of spring in 1945, the people of Berlin emerged from their air raid shelters to find devastation," Reagan said, carefully avoiding the obvious: American bombers were responsible for a good portion of that devastation. "Thousands of miles away, the people of the United States reached out to help." The Marshall Plan, named for Secretary of State George C. Marshall, provided the assistance to allow West Germany and West Berlin to emerge from the ashes of defeat, Reagan noted. The two enemies became friends and allies not after decades or even years of reconciliation, but almost immediately.

As a result, West Germany and West Berlin experienced nothing short of an economic miracle in the 1950s and '60s. The message was clear: through their alliance with the United States, Germans in the West enjoyed an astonishing reconstruction that brought prosperity, stability, and peace. "Where there was want," Reagan said, "today there's abundance—food, clothing, automobiles … From devastation, from utter ruin, you Berliners have, in freedom, built a city that once again ranks as one of the greatest on Earth. The Soviets may have had other plans," he said, moving his speech, as Kennedy did, from a tribute to Berlin to a condemnation of Communism on the other side of the wall. "But, my friends, there were a few things the Soviets didn't count on: Berliner herz, Berliner humor, ja, und Berliner schnauze." (In English, "Berlin's heart, Berlin's humor, and, of course, Berlin's wit.") The crowd ate up Reagan's tribute, his own humor, and even his attempts at German. They were prepared now for the heart of Reagan's speech: his angry confrontation with the wall and all that it represented.

The Soviets, he conceded, were making advances as never before. "Some political prisoners have been released," he said. "Certain foreign news broadcasts are no longer being jammed. Some economic enterprises have been permitted to operate with greater freedom from state control." The question, for Reagan, was whether these were "token gestures" or whether real reform was at hand.

The answer could be found in Berlin.

Reagan's voice was passionate, as Kennedy's was a quarter-century earlier. He remembered the sight of well-armed police ushering East Berliners away from the wall, away from the loudspeakers that would carry his words beyond the city's dividing line. "There is one sign the Soviets can make that would be unmistakable, that would advance dramatically the cause of freedom and peace," Reagan said. "General Secretary Gorbachev, if you seek peace, if you seek prosperity for the Soviet Union and Eastern Europe, if you seek liberalization, come here to this gate!

"Mr. Gorbachev, open this gate.

"Mr. Gorbachev, tear down this wall!"

The crowd erupted. Reagan's speech was not over; in fact, he was not even halfway through his prepared text. There was more to come: a tribute to the Western alliance that held firm during the protests against Reagan's missile deployment, a pledge to bring more international meetings to Berlin, and a request to bring the Olympic Games to Berlin, east and west. They were noble sentiments, but they lacked the power of the line that made the speech a classic piece of Reaganesque rhetoric.

He turned to the theme at the speech's conclusion, and in yet another echo of Kennedy, who finished his own speech with a vision of an undivided Berlin, Reagan quoted from a piece of graffiti sprayed on the wall: "'This wall will fall. Beliefs become reality.' Yes, across Europe this wall will fall," he said, more composed now than he had been. "For it cannot withstand faith; it cannot withstand truth. The wall cannot withstand freedom."

Ronald Reagan speaks at the Berlin Wall, Brandenburg Gate

Gerald Ford speaks on behalf of Robert Bork during Senate confirmation hearings on Bork's nomination to the U.S. Supreme Court

CHAPTER 27

Borked

Address to the Nation on the
Nomination of Robert Bork to the Supreme Court
October 14, 1987

TRACK 27

RONALD REAGAN USED HIS FIRST SUPREME COURT NOMINATION TO MAKE history: in 1981, Sandra Day O'Connor became the first woman appointed to the nation's highest court. Reagan's second chance to put his stamp on the Court came in 1986, when Warren Burger retired as chief justice. Reagan nominated Associate Justice William Rehnquist, like Burger a Nixon appointee, to be the new chief justice, and made history again by nominating Antonin Scalia to fill the vacancy created by Burger's retirement. Scalia was the first Italian American to serve on the high court.

In the summer of 1987, Reagan received another chance to move the Court to the right when Associate Justice Lewis Powell announced his retirement. The standard vetting process swung into motion to identify potential replacements, but one name already was on Reagan's mind: Robert Bork, a federal appeals court judge in Washington DC, and a well-known conservative intellectual who seemed to revel in ideological combat.

Thus far, Reagan had not had a problem winning Senate confirmation of his nominees. Both O'Connor and Scalia breezed through their confirmation votes, even though Scalia clearly was far more ideological than the moderate O'Connor. Rehnquist's promotion to chief justice faced a tougher hurdle when Senator Edward Kennedy revealed that Rehnquist owned property in a development that had a restrictive covenant that prohibited property sales to Jews. Rehnquist explained that he was unaware of the covenant, and while he won confirmation, thirty-three senators voted against him.

Reagan announced his choice of Bork on July 1, a few weeks after his return from Europe and a few days after another round of congressional hearings into Iran-Contra. In making his choice known, Reagan described Bork as "the most prominent and intellectually powerful advocate of judicial restraint in the country." There was no question about Bork's intellectual firepower or his qualifications. His personal life was in order; his closets were skeleton-free. Critics would not find anything scandalous in his conduct, and could not begin to assert that he was not qualified for the position.

Bork was a judge in the model of Scalia, whose Supreme Court nomination won unanimous Senate approval. Although the Senate was now in Democratic hands—Republicans were in the majority when Scalia came up for a vote—there was little reason to believe that Bork would face serious opposition. The Senate traditionally considered the qualifications and integrity of Supreme Court nominees, not their political views.

But in the summer of 1987, Ronald Reagan was a weakened president because of Iran-Contra, and Democrats were eager to seize an opportunity to counterattack as the presidential campaign of 1988 began to take shape. Bork was a tempting target. He was brilliant, but not lovable. His views were very much to the right, but he lacked Reagan's embracing demeanor and his amiability. And not a few Democrats remembered that he played an inglorious role during the Watergate scandal when he fired special prosecutor Leon Jaworski at the behest of an embattled Richard Nixon in 1973. Bork was the nation's solicitor general at the time, the third-ranking official at the Justice Department. His two immediate superiors, Attorney General Elliot Richardson and his top deputy, William Ruckelshaus, quit rather than do the deed. Bork had no such scruples, and did as Nixon wished.

Still, Bork's role in Watergate clearly was not enough to stop his nomination. His experience and credentials were beyond question. If Democrats wished to make an issue of his nomination, their argument would have to be based not on Bork's qualifications, but on his opinions.

And Bork had plenty of them, expressed in the forthright, vigorous language of an ideologue, not a consensus-builder. Because Bork's name had been suggested for the opening that went to Scalia in 1986, Democrats were prepared for battle when Reagan put his name forward.

July 1, 1987, was the beginning of no mere confirmation fight, but of a cultural war of astonishing vehemence. Senator Edward Kennedy of Massachusetts fired the first shots with his reaction to Bork's nomination. "Robert Bork's America," Kennedy said, "is a land in which women would be forced into back-alley abortions, blacks would sit at segregated lunch counters, rogue police could break down citizens' doors in midnight raids, school children could not be taught about evolution, writers and artists could be censored at the whim of government, and the doors of the federal courts would be shut on the fingers of millions of citizens for whom the judiciary is, and is often the only, protector of the individual rights that are the heart of democracy."[1]

It was a breathtaking condemnation the likes of which had seldom been heard in the generally polite politics of Supreme Court appointments. Bork's supporters, the president included, were stunned. Democratic activists, on the other hand, took Kennedy's comments as a rallying cry.

The battle of Robert Bork was underway.

Democrats intent on fighting and possibly blocking Bork's nomination found a way to turn the nominee's very strength—his years as a judge and his portfolio of opinions—into a weakness. Bork was no mere cipher. He had argued against legislation that banned racial discrimination in places of public accommodation, like lunch counters; he opposed the Court's intervention against political gerrymandering that gave excessive weight to some voters while diluting the votes of others, and he vehemently argued against the Court's landmark decision in *Roe v. Wade*, which legalized abortion. His views on abortion became the flashpoint for Democratic senators and liberal activists who launched a high-profile campaign against him. His supporters, taken aback by the Democratic strategy of attack, were slow to respond.

Reagan, in fact, was not in a position to respond. He was on a prolonged vacation in California, away from Iran-Contra, away from the confrontational politics his nominee had inspired. As critics on the Senate Judiciary Committee prepared to confront Bork, Reagan was thousands of miles away, unaware of the storm that was brewing in the Senate office building and in the headquarters of liberal activist groups that smelled blood, and victory, for the first time since Ronald Reagan set up shop at 1600 Pennsylvania Avenue.

Bork endured five days of questioning from the Senate Judiciary Committee, chaired by Delaware Senator Joseph Biden, a young dynamo with presidential ambitions. It was clear that the Democrats were intent on blocking Bork based not on his qualifications, but on his views—a strategy that was proving successful. As the hearings were wrapping up, Republican Senator Bob Packwood of Oregon announced that he planned to vote against Bork, a significant defection.

Reagan, back in Washington, was becoming uncharacteristically, and very publicly, angry. During a speech in New Jersey, he charged that Bork's critics were turning the confirmation process "into a political joke."[2] But neither Reagan nor the Democrats were laughing, for the process had turned ugly indeed. Bork's views were strong, and there was no question that he opposed abortion rights, but his views on civil rights legislation and other issues often were distorted or caricatured—in the same way that Reagan had often distorted or caricatured the views of some Democrats over the years. For Reagan's critics, it was payback time.

In early October, the Senate Judiciary Committee voted against confirmation, a deathblow to Bork's nomination. Not even Ronald Reagan's charm and persuasive powers were capable of reviving the nomination in the full Senate. Washington waited to hear word that the president would withdraw the nomination.

He chose an honorable defeat over ignominious surrender. With Bork's support, Reagan said he would not withdraw the nomination, but that he would press forward with a vote in the Senate. Every senator, then, would have to make a choice, and Reagan wanted that choice on the record. There would be no ducking Robert Bork.

Although the outcome was obvious, Reagan decided to take his case to the nation. On October 14, less than a week after the committee's vote, the president delivered a televised speech explaining why he would insist on a vote in the Senate. He did not speak in prime time, as was customary, but at 3:15 p.m., Washington time. The time slot indicated that Reagan knew he could not influence the outcome. He just wanted to fight.

"As you know," he said, "I have selected one of the finest judges in America's history, Robert Bork, for the Supreme Court. You've heard that this nomination is a lost cause. You've also heard that I am determined to fight down to the final ballot on the Senate floor. I am doing this because what's now at stake in this battle must never in our land of freedom become a lost cause. And whether lost or not, we Americans must never give up this particular battle: the independence of our judiciary."

But it was not Constitutional principle that motivated Reagan as much as it was personal animus for Bork's critics. He made that clear as he addressed the attacks on Bork. His soft inflections gave way to a hard edge as he continued. "Back in July when I nominated Judge Bork," he said, "I thought the confirmation process would go forward with a calm and sensible exchange of views. Unfortunately, the confirmation process became an ugly spectacle, marred by distortions and innuendos, and casting aside the normal rules of decency and honesty."

But while the campaign had been intensely personal, Reagan cast the debate as part of a larger conservative struggle against what he saw as a lenient court system that, he implied, Bork's critics supported. "After years of rising crime and leniency in the courtrooms," he said, addressing himself directly to his audience, "you demanded fair but tough law enforcement … And with your support, we've been able to turn things around in Washington." His choice of Bork, he said, was part of his effort to find judges who would "protect the rights of those who become victims of crime."

Reagan portrayed the controversy as a contest over crime and punishment, not about civil rights or the right to abortion. He avoided those issues entirely.

"So, my agenda is your agenda, and it's quite simple: to appoint judges like Judge Bork who don't confuse the criminals with the victims; judges who don't invent new or fanciful Constitutional rights for these criminals …"

He asked his viewers, and there were not many of them, not in the middle of the afternoon, to rally behind his nominee in hopes of persuading senators to change their minds. "Remind them that there is a thing we call the Constitution and to serve under it is a sacred trust, that they have sworn themselves to that trust … Now is the time to uphold that trust, no matter how powerful are those in opposition."

The speech had no soaring passages, no sunny tributes to the American spirit. It was an angry speech, delivered by a man struggling to persuade

Washington that he still was relevant, that he was not prepared to cede the rest of his time in office to caretakers on his staff.

In the end, of course, the speech was ineffective, as Reagan knew it must be. The Senate rejected Bork on October 23. Worse yet, Reagan's second choice, Douglas Ginsburg, was forced to withdraw when the press reported that he had used marijuana while in college. Reagan's third choice, Anthony Kennedy, ended the debacle.

Democrats and their supporters had won a rare victory, and the legacy of that victory influenced judicial politics in the years to come, for better or worse. During the fracas, Bork had said, "The tactics and techniques of national political campaigns have been unleashed on the process of confirming judges. That is not simply disturbing; it is dangerous. Federal judges are not appointed to decide cases according to the latest opinion polls; they are appointed to decide cases impartially, according to law." Yet the political intrigue would continue. Reagan's successor, George H.W. Bush, very carefully selected two Supreme Court justices, David Souter and Clarence Thomas, who had a modest paper trail. While Souter sailed through confirmation, Thomas's nomination led to one of the most memorable cultural exchanges of the 1990s when a lawyer named Anita Hill accused the nominee of sexual harassment, and Thomas replied that he felt he was subjected to what he called a "high-tech lynching." Thomas won nomination despite the controversy.

There was more bad news for President Reagan in the fall of 1987. Even while the Bork nomination reached its bitter climax, Wall Street was in disarray. The stock market sputtered in early October and finally crashed on October 19, five days after Reagan's speech about Bork.

Ronald Reagan with Robert Bork

Ronald Reagan speaks at Moscow State University

CHAPTER 28

A New World

Remarks to Students and
Faculty at Moscow State University
May 31, 1988

TRACK 28

IN THE EVENING OF RONALD REAGAN'S YEARS IN THE WHITE HOUSE, THE WORLD changed, and it moved in the very direction Reagan predicted it would back when his administration was young. In his letter to Leonid Brezhnev in 1981, he had asked the aging Soviet leader to imagine a world without nuclear weapons. He had told his audience in Britain in 1982 that he had a plan that would leave Marxism-Leninism "on the ash heap of history." He never seemed to doubt that the Soviet Union—the "evil empire"—would prove unable to resist the march of freedom and reform.

Now, as his presidency neared its final days, Ronald Reagan's dreams were on the verge of becoming reality. Mikhail Gorbachev introduced unprecedented reforms in a desperate attempt to revive the Soviet economy, he welcomed Reagan as a partner in arms reduction, and he seemed intent on achieving genuine change in the Communist state. All the while, the Soviet Union was collapsing. The Cold War was nearing a sudden and unexpected end.

On December 7, 1987, Gorbachev landed in Washington for a summit meeting with his new friend, Ronald Reagan. It was their first meeting since Reykjavík, when the two men left each other angry and embittered. But whatever their disagreements over missile defense, the two leaders needed each other. Gorbachev was trying to keep his country together; Reagan was trying to keep his presidency relevant. Both needed a dramatic, historic success, and they achieved it: agreement on a treaty to destroy hundreds of intermediate-range nuclear weapons in Europe. Among the missiles designated for destruction were the Soviet SS-20s and the American Pershing II and cruise missiles—the very weapons that set off the arms race of the late 1970s and early 1980s. Gorbachev came to Washington to sign the treaty and to celebrate the warmest relations between East and West since the end of World War II. The treaty passed the Senate several months later.

Gorbachev's visit was a brilliant success. He was so very different from past Soviet leaders: he smiled, he had style, he could banter like an American politician on the campaign trail, and he seemed to enjoy the public spectacle of politics. Washington in the fall of 1987 was worn down by Iran-Contra. The Reagan White House seemed to have lost its luster, and its direction. The country itself was falling into recession in the aftermath of October's stock market crash. Gorbachev was a welcome bit of fresh air.

The two men signed the Intermediate Nuclear Force (INF) treaty during a formal ceremony in the White House on December 8. The men and their aides then began their meetings. During a private moment, Reagan told Gorbachev he wanted one more summit before he left office, this one in Moscow. The Soviet leader agreed. In a more formal session, Gorbachev also agreed to let Reagan be Reagan—the president once again insisted that the United States would develop a missile defense system, and Gorbachev told him to go right ahead. He no longer viewed the system as a threat, because he believed it could never work, that it was doomed to be a colossal waste of money and resources.

Publicly, the highlight of the visit took place on December 10, when Gorbachev spontaneously stopped his motorcade, which was taking him to the White House from the Soviet Embassy, got out of his limousine, and plunged into a crowd of startled Americans strolling along Connecticut Avenue. It was a moment like no other in Cold War history. Gorbachev worked the crowd with smiles and handshakes, to the delight of those who happened to be passing by. News cameras recorded the chaotic, but happy, scene of Americans encircling the Soviet leader, sticking out their hands and pushing against each other to catch a glimpse or to make eye contact. Reagan watched the coverage on live television. The old performer couldn't help but admire Gorbachev's stunt. He told a reporter, "Wait until next summer and he sees what I do with his people."[1]

His chance came in late May 1988.

The final year of a two-term president rarely produces drama or memorable achievements. News at home is dominated not by the soon-to-be former president, but by the candidates who wish to take the president's place. In Ronald Reagan's case, however, it was clear that history would not and could not pause while America chose a new president. The Cold War was coming to a close. And for that reason, Ronald Reagan still mattered; indeed, he mattered more than ever before. The avowed anti-Communist, anti-Soviet ideologue accepted as his partner—as his friend—the general secretary of the Soviet Communist Party, Mikhail Gorbachev; together, the two were managing an end to more than four decades of a frightening and costly global rivalry.

Ronald Reagan landed in Moscow on May 29, 1988, for his first visit to the Soviet Union. The world had continued to change at remarkable speed since Gorbachev's visit to Washington in December. The Soviets announced their intention to withdraw from Afghanistan, signaling a recognition that the war there was done, and they had lost. In late March, the Sandinista government in Nicaragua and the Reagan-backed Contras agreed on a cease-fire. At home, Iran-Contra continued to reverberate, as Oliver North, John Poindexter, and others were indicted on a variety of charges relating to the scandal.

Whatever the final year of the Reagan presidency brought, few could argue that the news cycle had passed by the White House.

Reagan and Gorbachev talked briefly when the president arrived at the Kremlin. Afterwards Reagan and his wife, Nancy, stole a page from Gorbachev. As their motorcade approached a trendy shopping area in Moscow, the Reagans told their security detail to stop their car. They got out and began mingling with Muscovites who were as astonished, and delighted, as the Washingtonians who had found themselves shaking hands with Gorbachev in December. "It was amazing how quickly the street was jammed curb to curb with people—warm, friendly people who couldn't have been more affectionate," Reagan wrote in his diary.[2]

The Soviet security guards were not quite as huggable. Reagan tried to hide his dismay as he watched police officers battering people who pressed too close to the Reagans. Some American reporters were among those on the wrong end of a police fist. "I've never seen such a brutal manhandling," Reagan wrote.3

The next few days were heavily scripted and mostly ceremonial, a symbolic summit more than a substantive one. In a sense, the Washington meeting was the dramatic end to the unlikely and storied partnership between Reagan and Gorbachev. Moscow was a curtain call, an epilogue. But away from the meetings and formal conversations, Ronald Reagan showed that he still was capable of giving a stirring performance, using words as his props and ideas as his weapons. On May 31, the president spoke to students and faculty at Moscow State University. The setting could not have been imagined, except perhaps by Reagan himself, even four years earlier. The room held a large mural depicting the triumph of the Russian Revolution, while a supersized bust of Lenin himself loomed over the president as he spoke. Reagan made no notice of the irony as he talked to the students and teachers not only about differences, but about similarities as well.

"Standing here before a mural of your revolution," he said, "I want to talk about a very different revolution that is taking place right now, quietly sweeping the globe without bloodshed or conflict. Its effects are peaceful, but they will fundamentally alter our world, shatter old assumptions, and reshape our lives ... It's been called the technological or information revolution, and as its emblem, one might take the tiny silicon chip, no bigger than a fingerprint. One of these chips has more computing power than a roomful of old-style computers."

That revolution, he said, would allow mankind to break through "the material conditions of existence to a world where man creates his own destiny." The revolution, whatever it was to be called, would bring not the harsh upheaval of the Industrial Revolution, but liberty.

"Freedom, it has been said, makes people selfish and materialistic, but Americans are one of the most religious peoples on Earth," he said. "Because they know that liberty, just as life itself, is not earned but a gift from God, they seek to share that gift with the world ... Democracy is less a system of government than it is a system to keep government limited ... a system of constraints on power to keep politics and government secondary to the important things in life, the true sources of value found only in family and faith."

Reagan said it was his "fervent hope" that the United States and the Soviets would continue their recent "constructive cooperation" so that peace became "an enduring goal, not a tactical stage for a continuing conflict." The Russian people, he said, knew the true cost of war, but so did Americans. He conjured shared memories of World War II and the millions of lives cut short.

The students in his audience were the children of the children of war. They had no personal memories of the conflict that cost the lives of twenty million Russians. They knew of the war, knew of its cost, but they were of a different generation.

"Your generation," he said, "is living in one of the most exciting, hopeful times in Soviet history. It is a time when the first breath of freedom stirs the air and the heart beats to the accelerated rhythm of hope, when the accumulated spiritual energies of a long silence yearn to break free.

"We do not know what the conclusion will be of this journey, but we're hopeful that the promise of reform will be fulfilled. In this Moscow spring, this May 1988, we may be allowed that hope: that freedom, like the fresh green sapling planted over Tolstoy's grave, will blossom forth at last in the rich fertile soil of your people and culture. We may be allowed to hope that the marvelous sound of a new opening will keep rising through, ringing through, leading to a new world of reconciliation, friendship, and peace."

His last words were in Russian: da blagoslovit vas gospod—God bless you.

Following the speech, students were given an opportunity to ask Reagan questions. In an era that had seen so many improbable things come true, this was yet another in a long list—students in a state school in Moscow freely quizzing the president of the United States. He was asked how students had changed in the United States, for which he had a witty reply: "When I was governor of California," he said, "I could start a riot just by going to a campus." The students laughed when they were supposed to laugh, lifting Reagan's spirits. "You're great!" he said. "Carry on." Another student asked about regional conflicts around the world, prompting Reagan to discuss the prospects for peace in Central America, Asia, and South Africa. He was asked if he would be willing to help search for "310 Soviet soldiers" listed as missing in action in Afghanistan. "We would like nothing better than that," he said, softly.

The questions continued, seven in all. They were not all softballs: one asked about the plight of Native Americans, while another accused the president of meeting with "a former collaborator with a Fascist" during a previous session with a group of Soviet dissidents. Reagan offered diplomatic answers, personal reminiscences, and the usual complement of amusing anecdotes. He left to laughter and an ovation.

The Cold War was no more.

Ronald Reagan and Mikhail Gorbachev sign the INF Treaty in the White House; with this treaty, both superpowers agreed to eliminate their intermediate- and short-range ballistic missiles

Ronald Reagan, George H.W. Bush, and Mikhail Gorbachev on Governor's Island, New York

CHAPTER 29

A City Upon a Hill

Farewell Address to the Nation
January 11, 1989

TRACK 29

N OT SINCE DWIGHT EISENHOWER, WHO WAS PRESIDENT FROM 1953 TO 1961, had a president served two full terms. The tenure of every chief executive since 1961—John Kennedy, Lyndon Johnson, Richard Nixon, Gerald Ford, and Jimmy Carter—had been cut short, by murder, unpopularity, scandal, or discontent.

As 1988 gave way to 1989, Ronald Reagan prepared to leave office after eight tumultuous years in the White House. During his watch, the presidency was restored to its larger-than-life presence in American life, and the institution itself was stabilized after a series of broken or failed administrations.

Reagan's vice president, George H.W. Bush, won the 1988 presidential contest in part thanks to the American public's enduring affection for the outgoing president, despite a recession that followed the stock market crash of October 1987, and despite the endless and troubling revelations related to Iran-Contra. Democrats tried to tie Bush to the slower economy and Iran-Contra, but to no avail. Reagan's tenure might have been tarnished, but not his persona: his approval ratings were improving after bottoming out at the height of Iran-Contra. When he addressed the Republican National Convention in New Orleans in August, Reagan's popularity in the polls was nearly 60 percent. He handed that legacy to his vice president, saying, "George, just one personal request: Just go out there and win one for the Gipper."

Bush did exactly that. For the third time in three tries, and for the fifth time in six elections, the Republican Party captured the White House that fall. But it was a very different Republican Party now, and a very different country, than it was when Richard Nixon won election in 1968 to begin the series of GOP victories. Ronald Reagan had entered the White House at a time when the nation seemed more unsure of itself than at any time since the Great Depression. Abroad, the nation's enemies seemed on the march, and at home, the vicious combination of inflation and unemployment caused many to wonder if the U.S. was in permanent decline.

With words and ideas, with an optimism that rarely flagged, Ronald Reagan insisted that the nation could do better. His prescription for change was drastic, and he reveled in it. He had not been elected, he said, to preside over the status quo. He believed in the power of conservative ideas, and he had the skills to communicate those beliefs to a public that was as impatient as he was with old ideas. He broke with his party's centrist tradition, one that dated to before World War II, and through force of personality and the power of language, he moved the country in a direction he envisioned.

The Reagan years were not without pain, especially for blue-collar workers caught in a transition from an industrial economy to a knowledge economy. Unemployment averaged about 7 percent during Reagan's tenure. But inflation had been tamed, to about 3 percent, and interest rates had been cut by half. The federal government was spending $200 billion more per year than it took in, but the return on that spending was an improved military that was able to respond quickly to the emergencies of the late 20th century.

Reagan also changed the political culture of Washington, with consequences he did not anticipate. His emphasis on ideology led to greater partisan divisions and a more confrontational political style. The fight over Robert Bork proved to be a foreshadowing of a new kind of politics, nastier and more personal, light-years removed from the respectful rivalry that Reagan enjoyed with Tip O'Neill, who retired in 1987.

But another, far more important, relationship had undergone an historic transformation, from antagonism to partnership. The United States under Ronald Reagan made its peace with the Soviet Communists led by

Mikhail Gorbachev. Some conservatives regarded that peace as little more than an American surrender. In their view, Gorbachev had played Reagan for an aging fool whose staff wanted to make history through Jimmy Carter-style accommodation. Reagan had been sent to Washington to banish such mushy thinking, but as his administration entered its final weeks, some voices on the right complained that the president had fallen victim to appeasers on his staff. As the historian John Patrick Diggins noted, some "hard-line conservatives" accused Reagan of "not wanting to win the Cold War."[1]

But as he prepared to return to California, Reagan considered the matter of victory or defeat moot. The Cold War was over. The Soviets had changed their ways and would continue to change. True, Mr. Gorbachev had not torn down that wall, not yet. Surely, though, that day was in sight. Besides, the winners of the Cold War, in Reagan's eyes, would not be the United States or the West. The winners would be the people who lived on the eastern side of the wall, on the wrong side of the Iron Curtain.

Gorbachev and Reagan held their last formal meeting on December 6, 1988, when the Soviet leader addressed the United Nations in New York. Reagan and Bush hosted a reception for Gorbachev on Governors Island in New York Harbor, but the visit was cut short when word reached New York that a terrible earthquake had struck the Soviet republic of Armenia. Tens of thousands were dead. Gorbachev immediately flew home. Three weeks later, on January 1, 1989, Ronald Reagan and Mikhail Gorbachev celebrated the new year and the impending end of their historic partnership by sending recorded greetings to each other's people. "I believe the world is safer than it was a year ago, and I pray it will be safer still a year from now," Reagan told his Soviet audience. "I wish you, the Soviet people, well in the New Year." Gorbachev used his message to thank the American people for their assistance after the Armenian disaster. Not since World War II had a Soviet leader accepted American humanitarian aid. "Seeing all this," Gorbachev said of the response to the earthquake, "one cannot help thinking that all people who live on this Earth, all of us, however different, are really one family."[2]

The remainder of Reagan's days in the White House was spent in ceremony. Unlike the transition between Carter and Reagan, dominated by the outgoing president's efforts to win freedom for the hostages in Iran, this one was uneventful. On January 6, Reagan released a statement of condolences over the death of Japan's Emperor Hirohito, the man who led his country into war with the United States on December 7, 1941. Reagan paid tribute to the dead leader's efforts at "reconstruction and reconciliation."[3]

Four days later, on January 10, Reagan saluted the man who declared that December 7, 1941, would "live in infamy." The president spoke at a ceremony marking the 50th anniversary of the founding of the Franklin Roosevelt Library in Hyde Park, New York. "Franklin Roosevelt was the first President I ever voted for, the first to serve in my lifetime that I regarded as a hero, and the first I ever actually saw," a nostalgic Reagan said. He was impressed, he remembered, by Roosevelt's "infectious optimism" and by his faith in "the ordinary American"—qualities so many Americans now associated with Reagan himself.[4]

On the afternoon of January 11, the last two remaining members of Reagan's original Cabinet, Secretary of State George Shultz and Housing Secretary Samuel Pierce, presented Reagan with a comfy chair to enjoy while in retirement. The rest of the Cabinet, along with President-elect Bush, posed for one last photo of the Reagan team. They stood and smiled in front of a roaring fireplace in the Cabinet Room, with a portrait of Dwight Eisenhower watching the proceedings from above the mantle. In response to a question from the press, Reagan insisted that, "I'm not retiring."[5]

Later that evening, Reagan seated himself behind his desk in the Oval Office for one last televised address to the American people. The speech had been in the works for several weeks, with former speechwriter Peggy Noonan brought in to craft a personal summation of an extraordinary era. Noonan later recounted her meetings with Reagan to biographer Richard Reeves, saying that the president wanted to focus on the nation's economic turnaround and its renewed high standing in the world. The speech, he implied, ought to be uplifting and optimistic—how, or why, could it have been anything else?

And so the Oval Office was prepared one last time for one of its greatest performers. As Reagan awaited his cue, scheduled for just after nine o'clock Washington time, he shuffled a paper copy of his speech. Heavy, ornate drapes, slightly parted in the middle, formed the backdrop, along with small family portraits barely visible over his shoulders. He wore his usual blue suit, with a red tie, and a white handkerchief in his breast pocket.

During his last few weeks in office, the president, just shy of his seventy-eighth birthday, seemed to slow down noticeably. Although physically fit, he looked tired. Washington whispered that President-elect Bush already was governing the country, that Reagan was a spent force.

But when it was time to begin speaking, the Reagan of old reappeared. The television audience saw an older but energetic president, wistful like a grandfather, but still seemingly not ready for a pair of slippers and that comfy chair.

He talked about the great view he had from one of the White House windows, where he could see the great monuments of Washington DC. If the humidity were low, he said, the view expanded beyond the Mall, to the Potomac River, where he sometimes saw a sailboat gliding by.

"I've been thinking a bit at that window," he said. "I've been reflecting on what the past eight years have meant and mean." The view, he said, reminded him of what a Chinese refugee had said to an American sailor when the refugee was rescued from the South China Sea. "He yelled, 'Hello, American sailor. Hello, freedom man.'

"A small moment with big meaning, a moment the sailor, who wrote it in a letter, couldn't get out of his mind. And, when I saw it, neither could I. Because that's what it was to be an American in the 1980s. We stood, again, for freedom. I know we always have, but in the past few years the world again—and in a way, we ourselves—rediscovered it. It's been quite a journey this decade, and we held together through some stormy seas. And at the end, together, we are reaching our destination."

It was a journey with many milestones: the recession and recovery of the early and mid '80s; Grenada; the summits with Gorbachev. Unable to resist a jab at critics, the president noted that many believed he chose the wrong course in 1981. "Some pundits said our programs would result in catastrophe," he said. They were wrong. "What they called 'radical' was really 'right.' What they called 'dangerous' was just 'desperately needed.'"

He noted that his campaign to change the nation's direction had won him the nickname, "The Great Communicator." It was, he said, a title he didn't deserve. "I wasn't a great communicator, but I communicated great things, and they didn't spring full bloom from my brow, they came from the heart of a great nation … They called it the Reagan revolution. Well, I'll accept that, but for me it always seemed more like the great rediscovery, a rediscovery of our values and our common sense."

He talked not only of the changes in America, but of those around the globe, where nations were "turning to free markets and free speech and turning away from the ideologies of the past." Among those nations was the Soviet Union, where, he said, Gorbachev was bringing about "internal democratic reforms." And that was why he was different. In his last speech as president, Ronald Reagan uttered words few could have imagined even four years earlier. "We must keep up our guard," he said, "but we must also continue to work together to lessen and eliminate tension and mistrust … I want the new closeness to continue." Of Gorbachev, he said, "We wish him well."

Extraordinary, indeed.

As he closed, Reagan turned inward in a way that he rarely did in his speeches from the Oval Office. Prodded by Noonan, he tried to express his vision of America, not just in 1989, but for all time. He returned to that view he had enjoyed so often from the White House window.

"The past few days," he said, "when I've been at that window upstairs, I've thought a bit of the 'shining city upon a hill.' The phrase comes from John Winthrop, who wrote it to describe the America he imagined. What he imagined was important because he was an early Pilgrim, an early freedom man.

"I've spoken of the shining city all my political life, but I don't know if I ever quite communicated what I saw when I said it. But in my mind it was a tall, proud city built on rocks stronger than oceans, wind-swept, God-blessed, and teeming with people of all kinds living in harmony and peace; a city with free ports that hummed with commerce and creativity. And if there had to be city walls, the walls had doors and the doors were open to anyone with the will and the heart to get here. That's how I saw it, and see it still.

"And how stands the city on this winter night? More prosperous, more secure, and happier than it was eight years ago … And she's still a beacon, still a magnet for all who must have freedom, for all the pilgrims from all the lost places who are hurtling through the darkness, toward home.

"We've done our part … My friends: We did it. We weren't just marking time. We made a difference. We made the city stronger, we made the city freer, and we left her in good hands. All in all, not bad, not bad at all."

That was it. His time as leader of the Free World was about to expire, but he left power as he entered it, with an appreciation for the power of words and imagery, with an ability to communicate great ideas in gripping language, and with an unshakable belief in his country's greatness, and goodness.

On January 20, 1989, Ronald Reagan returned to the west side of the Capitol to watch his vice president and successor, George H.W. Bush, take the oath of office. In a rare gesture, Bush shared a moment of his day in the sun with his predecessor. "There is a man here who has earned a lasting place in our hearts and in our history," Bush said in the opening minute of his inaugural address. "President Reagan, on behalf of our nation, I thank you for the wonderful things that you have done for America."

The crowd erupted in applause. Reagan waved his hand, and the moment was gone—it was time to move on. In a matter of hours, Ronald Reagan was in a helicopter with his wife, flying over the White House one last time. "Look, honey," he said to Nancy as he pointed to their home for eight years, "there's our little shack."[6]

He was on his way back to California, and into the pages of history.

Ronald Reagan salutes as he boards the helicopter at the U.S. Capitol on January 20, 1989, his last day as president

Epilogue

The Sunset of My Life

He lived to see the wall torn down, not by Mr. Gorbachev, but by ordinary men and women who yearned for the freedom Ronald Reagan championed. He lived to see the Soviet Union fall, and with it, an end to Communist domination of Eastern Europe. He lived to see a peaceful end to the Cold War, to the triumph of the values he celebrated during a long and memorable public life. In the fall of 1990, Ronald Reagan traveled to Westminster College in Missouri, where, in 1946, Winston Churchill drew the world's attention to the Soviet imprisonment of Eastern Europe. "From Stettin in the Baltic to Trieste in the Adriatic, an iron curtain has descended across the continent," Churchill had roared.

Now, it was Ronald Reagan's turn to bookend Churchill's speech with one of his own, to celebrate the end of the Cold War by dedicating a Cold War monument on the campus where, in a way, the Cold War began. His speech was triumphant where Churchill's was defiant, reflective where Churchill's was prophetic, a speech that closed an era that began, rhetorically anyway, with Churchill's coining of the phrase "Iron Curtain."

"His Fulton speech was a firebell in the night," Reagan said, "a Paul Revere warning that tyranny was on the march ... Out of one man's speech was born a new Western resolve."

Reagan embodied that resolve. His speech to the British Parliament in 1982 and his evil empire speech in Florida in 1983 were the rhetorical successors of Churchill's Iron Curtain speech, works of moral clarity and firmly held conviction whose truths, years later, seemed indisputable. "I was by no means alone," Reagan told his audience. "Principled leaders like Helmet Kohl and Margaret Thatcher reinforced our message …"

It was American leadership, however, that helped bring about an end to a conflict that defined an age. Reagan, in this moment of victory and vindication, paid tribute to the nation he led for eight years. Nearing his eightieth birthday, his enthusiasm for the land of his birth, his sunny view of its future, and his belief in its exceptional place in the narrative of world history, remained undiminished. "The truth of the matter is, if we take this crowd and if we could go through and ask the heritage, the background of every family here, we would probably come up with the names of every country on earth … Here is the one spot on earth where we have the brotherhood of man."

The Westminster College speech was one of Ronald Reagan's last memorable public appearances. Television viewers caught glimpses of him in April 1994, when he was among five presidents—Bill Clinton, George H.W. Bush, Gerald Ford, and Jimmy Carter—who gathered in California for the funeral of a sixth, Richard Nixon. The public didn't see, couldn't see, Ronald Reagan's diminished faculties. Seven months later, on November 5, 1994, he wrote a letter in his own hand to the American people, informing them that he had been diagnosed with the illness that killed his mother, Alzheimer's disease.

He chose to acknowledge the disease, he wrote, in hopes "that this might promote greater awareness of this condition." Both the former president and his wife, Nancy, had very public bouts with cancer, and believed their candor helped others take steps to prevent the disease, or cope with it when it was diagnosed.

He said he felt fine and that he planned to "continue to share in life's journey" with Nancy and his family, although he acknowledged that as time passed, his family would face emotional burdens they could not imagine.

"When the Lord calls me home, whenever that may be, I will face it with the greatest love for this country of ours and eternal optimism for its future," he wrote.

"I now begin the journey that will lead me into the sunset of my life. I know that for America there will always be a bright dawn ahead."

The sun set on Ronald Reagan's life on June 5, 2004, ninety-three years after his birth. As the disease progressed, he disappeared from American life, but his supporters began campaigns to memorialize him even before he slipped away. He was unaware of the testimonials and displays of affection; Nancy Reagan told author Richard Reeves that her husband did not open his eyes during his last four years.

He received a state funeral in Washington, the first for a president since John Kennedy's in 1963, and he was buried in California. His eight years in Washington profoundly affected the times in which we live. His words and his ideas defined the times in which he lived. They are still discussed, still quoted, still remembered. Because they still matter.

Notes

Introduction
[1] Ronald Reagan, *An American Life*, 115.

Part I

Chapter One
[1] Reagan, *An American Life*, 105.
[2] Ibid., 143.
[3] Ibid., 141.
[4] Ibid., 106.
[5] Ibid., 120.

Chapter Two
[1] Reagan, *An American Life*, 150.

Chapter Four
[1] Lou Cannon, *Reagan*, 253.
[2] Ibid., 267.

Chapter Five
[1] Cannon, *Reagan*, 274.

Part II

Chapter Six
[1] Richard Reeves, *President Reagan*, 2.
[2] Ibid., 2.
[3] Ibid., 2.
[4] Reagan, *An American Life*, 20–21.

Chapter Seven
[1] www.reagan.utexas.edu/archives/speeches/1981/20581c.htm.

[2] Reeves, *President Reagan*, 34.

[3] Ibid., 35.

[4] Reagan, *An American Life*, 260.

[5] Reeves, *President Reagan*, 38.

[6] Reagan, *An American Life*, 263.

[7] Reeves, *President Reagan*, 56.

[8] John A. Farrell, *Tip O'Neill and the Democratic Century*, 556.

[9] Reagan, *An American Life*, 288.

Chapter Eight

[1] Reagan, *An American Life*, 131.

[2] Ibid., 283.

Chapter Nine

[1] Reeves, *President Reagan*, 99.

[2] Reagan, *An American Life*, 269.

[3] Ibid., 270.

[4] John Patrick Diggins, *Ronald Reagan: Fate, Freedom, and the Making of History*, 191.

[5] Reagan, *An American Life*, 272.

[6] Ibid., 273.

Chapter Eleven

[1] Cannon, *President Reagan: The Role of a Lifetime*, 271.

[2] Reagan, *An American Life*, 315.

[3] Cannon, *President Reagan*, 348.

[4] Reagan, *An American Life*, 321.

[5] Ibid., 322.

[6] Ibid., 322.

Chapter Twelve

[1] Cannon, *President Reagan*, 805.

[2] Ibid., 318.

Chapter Thirteen

[1] Reagan, *An American Life*, 550.

2 Ibid., 547.

3 Ibid., 550.

4 Cannon, *President Reagan*, 321.

5 Martin Anderson, *Revolution: The Reagan Legacy*, 73.

6 Ibid., 79.

7 Ibid., 82–83.

8 Cannon, *President Reagan*, 329.

Chapter Fourteen
1 Reagan, *An American Life*, 477.

2 Ibid., 477.

3 Reeves, *President Reagan*, 153.

4 Reeves, *President Reagan*, 153.

Chapter Fifteen
1 Cannon, *President Reagan*, 314.

2 Reeves, *President Reagan*, 168.

3 Reagan, *An American Life*, 583.

4 Ibid., 585.

5 Ibid., 586.

Chapter Sixteen
1 Cannon, *President Reagan*, 401.

2 Reagan, *An American Life*, 437.

3 Ibid., 443.

4 Ibid., 443.

Chapter Eighteen
1 Cannon, *President Reagan*, 516.

2 Garry Wills, *Reagan's America*, 231.

3 Reagan, *An American Life*, 327.

4 Wills, *Reagan's America*, 231.

5 Reeves, *President Reagan*, 233.

Part III

Chapter Nineteen

1 Reagan, *An American Life*, 490.

Chapter Twenty

1 Reagan, *An American Life*, 377.
2 Cannon, *President Reagan*, 580.
3 Reagan, *An American Life*, 379.

Chapter Twenty-One

1 Cannon, *President Reagan*, 554.
2 Reagan, *An American Life*, 306.
3 Ibid., 335.
4 Reagan, *An American Life*, 335.

Chapter Twenty-Two

1 Diggins, *Ronald Reagan*, 365.
2 www.reagan.utexas.edu/archives/speeches/1986/12586a.htm.
3 Cannon, *President Reagan*, 499.
4 Reagan, *An American Life*, 403.
5 www.reagan.utexas.edu/archives/speeches/1986/12886a.htm.
6 Reeves, *President Reagan*, 308.
7 Tip O'Neill with William Novak, *Man of the House*, 363.

Chapter Twenty-Three

1 Reagan, *An American Life*, 515.
2 Ibid., 518.
3 Ibid., 518.
4 Reeves, *President Reagan*, 319.
5 www.reagan.utexas.edu/archives/speeches/1986/40986d.htm.
6 Reagan, *An American Life*, 518.
7 Ibid., 519.

Chapter Twenty-Four

1 Reagan, *An American Life*, 123.

2 Ibid., 170.

3 Reeves, *President Reagan*, 456.

4 Ibid., 13.

5 Jane Mayer and Doyle McManus, *Landslide: The Unmaking of a President*, 280.

Chapter Twenty-Five

1 Reagan, *An American Life*, 502.

2 Cannon, *President Reagan*, 610.

3 Reeves, *President Reagan*, 269.

4 Reagan, *An American Life*, 528.

5 www.reagan.utexas.edu/archives/speeches/1986/111386c.htm.

6 Reagan, *An American Life*, 530.

7 Reeves, *President Reagan*, 382.

Chapter Twenty-Six

1 Reagan, *An American Life*, 677.

2 Reeves, *President Reagan*, 401.

3 Ibid., 401.

Chapter Twenty-Seven

1 Ethan Bronner, *Battle for Justice: How the Bork Nomination Shook America*, 98.

2 Reeves, *President Reagan*, 422.

Chapter Twenty-Eight

1 Reeves, *President Reagan*, 442.

2 Reagan, *An American Life*, 709.

3 Ibid., 709.

Chapter Twenty-Nine

1 Diggins, *Ronald Reagan*, 418.

2 www.reagan.utexas.edu/archives/speeches/1989/010189a.htm.

3 www.reagan.utexas.edu/archives/speeches/1989/010689i.htm.

4 www.reagan.utexas.edu/archives/speeches/1989/011089c.htm.

5 www.reagan.utexas.edu/archives/speeches/1989/011189e.htm.

6 Reagan, *An American Life*, 724.

Bibliography

Anderson, Martin. *Revolution: The Reagan Legacy*. (San Diego: Harcourt, Brace, Jovanovich, 1988).

Beschloss, Michael R. and Strobe Talbott. *At the Highest Levels: The Inside Story of the End of the Cold War*. (Boston: Back Bay Books, 1994).

Bronner, Ethan. *Battle for Justice: How the Bork Nomination Shook America*. (New York: Union Square Books, 2007).

Cannon, Lou. *Reagan*. (New York: G. P. Putnam's Sons, 1982).

———. *President Reagan: The Role of a Lifetime*. (New York: Simon & Schuster, 1991).

Dallek, Mathew. *The Right Moment*. (New York: Oxford University Press, 2004).

Dallek, Robert. *Ronald Reagan: The Politics of Symbolism*. (Cambridge: Harvard University Press, 1984).

Diggins, John Patrick. *Ronald Reagan: Fate, Freedom, and the Making of History*. (New York: W. W. Norton, 2007).

Farrell, John A. *Tip O'Neill and the Democratic Century*. (Boston: Little, Brown, 2001).

LaFeber, Walter. *Inevitable Revolutions: The United States in Central America*. (New York: W. W. Norton, 1993).

Mayer, Jane and Doyle McManus. *Landslide: The Unmaking of a President, 1984–1988*. (Boston: Houghton Mifflin, 1988).

Noonan, Peggy. *When Character Was King: A Story of Ronald Reagan*. (New York: Penguin, 2002).

O'Neill, Thomas P. with William Novak. *Man of the House: The Life and Political Memoirs of Speaker Tip O'Neill*. (New York: Random House, 1987).

Reagan, Ronald. *An American Life*. (New York: Pocket Books, 1999).

Reeves, Richard. *President Reagan: The Triumph of Imagination*. (New York: Simon & Schuster, 2005).

Stockman, David A. *The Triumph of Politics: Why the Reagan Revolution Failed*. (New York: Harper & Row, 1986).

Wills, Garry. *Reagan's America: Innocents at Home*. (New York: Penguin, 1988).

Index

Credits

Audio and photos courtesy of the Ronald Reagan Presidential Foundation and the Miller Center of Public Affairs at the University of Virginia.

Additional photos copyright The Associated Press on pages: 11*right* (AP Photo), 12 (AP Photo/Anthony Camerano), 32 (AP Photo/J. Walter Green), 39 (AP Photo/White House, Courtesy Gerald R. Ford Library, William Fitz-Patrick), 48 (AP Photo), 82 (AP Photo/Str), 90 (AP Photo/Ron Edmonds), 102 (AP Photo/Boris Yurchenko), 118 (AP Photo/Arturo Robles), 126 (AP Photo/Barry Thumma), 133 (AP Photo/Mikami), 157 *left* (AP Photo/Scott Stewart), 174 (AP Photo/Scott Stewart), 180 *top* (AP Photo/NASA), 180 *bottom* (AP Photo/Bruce Weaver), 188 (AP Photo/Arna of Tripoli), 218 (AP Photo/Charles Tasnadi).

Audio segments have been edited for time and content. In the interest of clarity and accuracy, all edits within each speech are made apparent by the fading out of the audio, then the fading in of the next segment. While we have attempted to achieve the best possible quality on this archival material, some audio quality is the result of source limitations. Audio denoising by Christian Pawola at Music & Sound Company, DeKalb, Illinois.

For full versions of most of the speeches featured in the book, plus a wealth of other information about the president, visit the website of the Ronald W. Reagan Library and Museum at http://www.reaganlibrary.net, or the Miller Center at millercenter.org/academic/americanpresident/reagan.

About Sourcebooks MediaFusion

Launched with the 1998 *New York Times* bestseller *We Interrupt This Broadcast* and formally founded in 2000, Sourcebooks MediaFusion is the nation's leading publisher of mixed-media books. This revolutionary imprint is dedicated to creating original content—be it audio, video, CD-ROM, or Web—that is fully integrated with the books we create. The result, we hope, is a new, richer, eye-opening, thrilling experience with books for our readers. Our experiential books have become both bestsellers and classics in their subjects, including poetry (*Poetry Speaks Expanded*), children's books (*Poetry Speaks to Children*), history (*Harlem Speaks*), sports (*Harry Caray: Voice of the Fans*), the plays of William Shakespeare, and more. See what's new from us at www.sourcebooks.com.

Acknowledgments

This book has been a wonderful collaboration with a number of talented people at Sourcebooks. My thanks to Todd Green, Stephen O'Rear, the Sourcebooks publicity staff, copyeditor Brenda Horrigan, and editor Hillel Black.

I also am grateful for the cooperation of the Ronald Reagan Presidential Foundation and Library and its chief of staff, Joanne Drake. The staffs of the foundation and library were extraordinarily generous with their time and resources.

As always, my thanks to John Wright. And, of course, to Eileen Duggan.

About the Author

© *William Tomlin*

Terry Golway is curator of the John Kean Center for American History at Kean University in Union, NJ. He is the author of *Washington's General*, a biography of Nathanael Greene, and co-author of *Let Every Nation Know*, a retrospective of John F. Kennedy's speeches. He writes for the *New York Times*, *America*, the *Irish Echo*, and the *New York Observer*. He lives in Maplewood, New Jersey.